# THE ARCHAEOLOGY OF ANCIENT TURKEY

A BODLEY HEAD ARCHAEOLOGY

# The Archaeology of Ancient Turkey

## JAMES MELLAART

*Drawings by*
**SHIRLEY FELTS**

*Maps by*
**EDGAR HOLLOWAY**

THE BODLEY HEAD · London Sydney Toronto

THE BODLEY HEAD ARCHAEOLOGIES
*Edited by* MAGNUS MAGNUSSON

MAGNUS MAGNUSSON *Introducing Archaeology*
*Viking Expansion Westwards*
T. G. H. JAMES *The Archaeology of Ancient Egypt*
RONALD HARKER *Digging Up the Bible Lands*
REYNOLD HIGGINS *The Archaeology of Minoan Crete*
JOHN HAY *Ancient China*
PAUL JOHNSTONE *The Archaeology of Ships*
BARRY CUNLIFFE *Rome and the Barbarians*
KENNETH HUDSON *The Archaeology of Industry*
PETER HARBISON *The Archaeology of Ireland*
DAVID BROWN *Anglo-Saxon England*

IN PREPARATION

DAVID RIDGWAY *The Origin of the Etruscans*

FRONTISPIECE
Relief of a warrior god
from the so-called
King's Gate, Hattusa.

British Library Cataloguing in Publication Data
Mellaart, James
The archaeology of ancient Turkey. —(The Bodley Head Archaeologies).
1. Excavations (Archaeology)—Turkey 2. Turkey—Antiquities
I. Title II. Series
939.2     DR431
ISBN 0-370-10842-6

© James Mellaart 1978
Drawings © The Bodley Head 1978
Printed in Great Britain for
The Bodley Head Ltd
9 Bow Street, London WC2E 7AL
by BAS Printers Limited,
Over Wallop, Hampshire
Set in Monophoto Ehrhardt
*First published in 1978*

# CONTENTS

# ACKNOWLEDGMENTS

I would like to dedicate this book to the great Turkish archaeologist, Hamit Zübeyr Koşay.

Thanks are due to the following for permission to reproduce black-and-white photographs: Hirmer Fotoarchiv, Munich, frontispiece and pages 40, 43, 55, 56, 68, 73, 82, 83 and 87; Peter Clayton, page 35; Norbert Schimmel, pages 64, 65 and 75; the University Museum of Pennsylvania, pages 85, 89 and 90; *Archaeometry*, 1971, page 25; Department of Antiquities, Cyprus, page 97; Birmingham Museums and Art Gallery, page 108.

For permission to use colour photographs thanks are due to *Archaeometry*, 1971, facing page 17 (*top*); Hirmer Fotoarchiv, Munich, facing pages 33, 64 and 65; Machteld Mellink, facing page 80 (*bottom*); University Museum of Pennsylvania, facing page 81 (*top and bottom*).

The line drawing on page 31 is based on one by Bernabo Brea; those on pages 36 and 37 are courtesy Donald Easton; the drawing on page 39 is based on one by Hamit Zübeyr Koşay; those on pages 49 and 100 are based on drawings by Tahsin Özgüc; those on pages 50 and 51 on drawings by Sedat Alp; that on page 52 on a drawing by Nimet Özgüc; that on page 77 on a drawing by Kurt Bittel; the drawing on page 86 appears by permission of the Pennsylvania University Museum; that on page 98 is courtesy of N. Taşyüzek; and that on page 103 on a drawing by Charles Burney.

Other photographs are by Arlette Mellaart and the property of the author.

The publishers have made every effort to trace the owners of copyright material appearing in this book. In the event of any question arising as to the use of such material, the publishers, while expressing regret for any error unconsciously made, will be pleased to make the necessary correction in any future edition.

# PREFACE

It was on a bright, sunny morning in November, 1952, that I got my first glimpse of the prehistoric settlement mound called Çatal Hüyük, near the edge of the Konya Plain in south-central Turkey. I did not know its name then, but even from nine kilometres away it looked distinctly inviting: the gentle slope with which it rose seventeen metres above the plain suggested that it could well be an early site. But I had no idea then that it would turn out to be the location of one of the earliest towns in the world, and that it would revolutionise all our thinking about the origins of civilisation in the Near East.

The Konya Plain is really a vast plateau ringed with extinct volcanoes which were last active in the second millennium BC. The plain itself, over 1,000 metres above sea-level, was once fertile grass- and steppe-land, but most of it is now semi-arid and covered with a thick pall of buff dust. It formed part of ancient Anatolia, which can be defined as the whole of western Turkey bounded by the crescent line of the Taurus Mountains that stretches from the Mediterranean to the western borders of Persia, plus Cilicia to the south-east.

When I first saw Çatal Hüyük, I had been working in southern Anatolia for two seasons, surveying prehistoric mounds by collecting samples of potsherds found on their surface. I had gone to Turkey in 1951 because I was hoping to discover the origins of those mysterious 'Sea-Peoples' who invaded the eastern Mediterranean around 1200 BC and settled on the coastal plain of Palestine as the 'Philistines'; I had an idea that they might have come from the shores of Asia Minor, and I wanted to see if there was any evidence to substantiate this theory.

Instead, I found hundreds of sites which were very much earlier than that—and much earlier than archaeologists in those days thought possible, dating far back into the Neolithic period (7500 to

6300 BC)* and Chalcolithic period (6300 to 4000 BC). By the time I glimpsed Çatal Hüyük, I had learned to recognise likely sites at a glance, and I was tempted to go and explore it. But the season for surveying was drawing to a close—in my first season the previous year, I had been caught unprepared by snow at the end of November, and in that exposed area it was an unpleasant experience. Çatal Hüyük was two hours' walk away, and there were a number of sites in the immediate vicinity that needed investigating as well. Besides, I had already taken samples of potsherds from several other sites that morning, and I did not relish carrying ten kilos of potsherds in my bags all that way and back to my base at the little market town of Çumra, before depositing them, after proper study, in the Konya Museum.

Since April I had been criss-crossing southern Turkey, mostly on foot because I couldn't afford to hire transport (my scholarship to the British Institute of Archaeology in Ankara was £250, which I wanted to last me two years). I had picked up dysentery in the Taurus Mountains in September, and it was still with me. I had already made a rich haul of finds that summer, and to be honest I felt a little depressed at the sight of how much there was left to do—there seemed to be prehistoric mounds stretching all around me as far as the horizon, and I knew I simply couldn't cover them all on foot.

So, a little reluctantly, I gave up the idea of going to Çatal Hüyük for the time being, finished off the sites nearer Çumra, and returned to Ankara to spend the winter studying and digesting what I had found. It was not to be until November, 1958, that I returned to Çatal Hüyük with a couple of friends who had a Land-Rover, and realised at a glance that it was the remains of a Neolithic city.

But by then we had already started an excavation at another site in south-western Anatolia, Hacılar, pushing our earliest record of the development of village settlement in Anatolia back to the start of the Neolithic period around 7500 BC—a full 4,500 years earlier than scholars had previously believed possible.

---

*Throughout this book I have used a high chronology for the prehistoric period based on calibrated C14 dating; for the historical period that proposed by Professors Landsberger and Nagel. The so-called Middle chronology now used in most standard reference books, like the *Cambridge Ancient History*, is not compatible with C14 datings.

# 1

# Çatal Hüyük: the Neolithic Revolution

It is always difficult to convince people that generally held beliefs are not necessarily correct; it therefore took years for the scholarly world to realise that, contrary to their beliefs, the Anatolian plateau had been inhabited from the start of the Neolithic period, that is to say, the period in which food production by farming began. No archaeological survey had been carried out on the plateau itself. At that time, only two sites had produced stratified sequences that reached back to the Neolithic period—Mersin and Tarsus; but these were in Cilicia, close to the Fertile Crescent, and were therefore considered as western outposts of Syria and Mesopotamia where the Fertile Crescent swung down into Syria—and a new term, 'Syro-Cilician', was coined to bolster that conviction. The Taurus Mountains to the north were taken to be the northern frontiers of the civilised world, and Anatolia's cultural development was regarded as backward. It was not supposed to have started before 3000 BC. Archaeological maps showed southern Anatolia as a great unexplored blank.

My three-year archaeological survey, 1951–3, replaced much of the blank area on the maps with hundreds of prehistoric sites. The vast majority of them emphasised the importance of southern Anatolia during the Bronze Age (4000 to 1200 BC); but many of the potsherds found on the surface of the mounds suggested much earlier occupation—the dark monochrome ware of the Neolithic period, the red on white painted ware of the Early Chalcolithic, and the white on dark painted ware of the Late Chalcolithic: enough, in fact, to indicate large numbers of previously unknown cultures. What was needed now was systematic excavation to put these finds into chronological

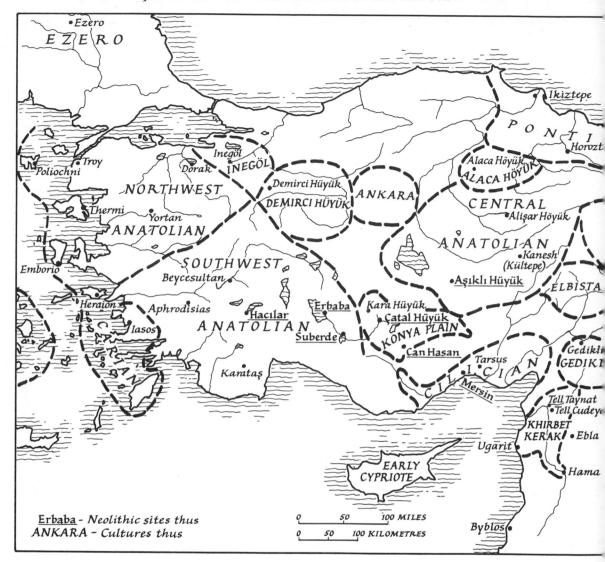

Neolithic and Early Bronze Age cultures and sites. The broken lines indicate cultural provinces.

perspective, and learn something of the way in which the makers of the pottery had lived, for archaeology deals with people and not just potsherds.

So in 1954 the British Institute of Archaeology at Ankara, under its then director, Seton Lloyd, and myself, started excavations at the big site of Beycesultan on the upper Meander River in south-western Turkey, one of the sites plotted during my 1952 survey.

Nothing earlier than the Late Chalcolithic (*c.* 5500–4000 BC) was found in a deep sounding that reached virgin soil twenty-six metres below the surface of the mound. Investigation of the later strata was carried on between 1954 and 1959, but I was even more interested in

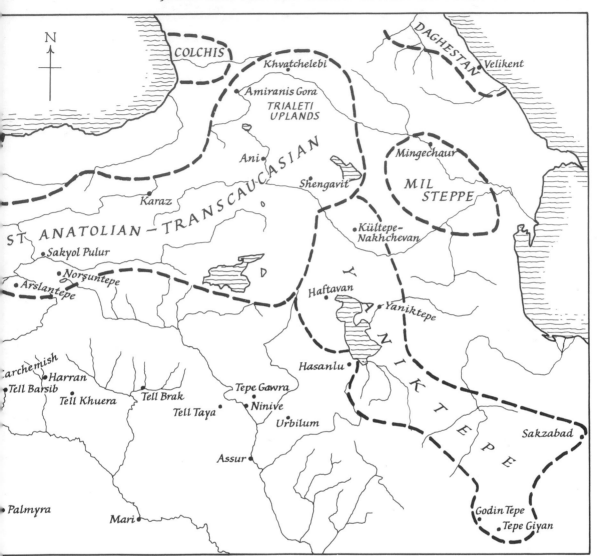

finding an earlier site. My search led me in 1956 to Burdur, where a local schoolteacher sent me to the village of Hacılar. Here, a peasant gave me two strangely decorated pots he had dug up. The trail led to a field beneath a rock bluff and alongside an orchard; and in the following year, 1957, I started the first of four seasons of excavation there.

In the course of the four years we found a great deal of highly sophisticated and gaily painted pottery that made the name 'Hacılar' celebrated throughout the archaeological world. It dated from the Early Chalcolithic (c. 6300–5650 BC), and will be dealt with in full in proper chronological order, in the next chapter. But with four days to go before the end of the final season, we came across evidence of a much earlier settlement period dating from about 7500 BC. This made the site as old as anything known in Mesopotamia, and vindicated my belief that Anatolia was no cultural backwater.

The architectural remains from this early village at Hacılar ('aceramic' or 'pre-pottery' Hacılar, as it is called) were relatively simple, and consisted of mud-brick walls on stone foundations, grouped along an open courtyard containing numerous hearths and ovens, grain-bins, and post-holes for awnings and sheds. The rooms were rectangular in plan, but there was no sign of doorways—so they must have been entered from the roof. Some of the walls were plastered and painted red, at least as a dado along the base. We found human skulls on some floors, which may suggest a form of ancestor worship. There were a few artefacts of stone, but no pottery was found. There were some animal bones, of cattle, deer, sheep and goat, but it was impossible to say with certainty that they were from animals that had been domesticated with one exception: dog. However, there was plenty of evidence of organised agriculture, with the seeds of two-row hulled barley, emmer wheat, wild einkorn, lentil, and several weeds.

The pre-pottery village at Hacılar was abandoned by its inhabitants, for some reason, for about a thousand years before the new settlement was built on top of it by the pottery-makers. I wanted a site which would fill in this hiatus of a thousand years, and the obvious choice was Çatal Hüyük.

I had eventually got round to surveying Çatal Hüyük in November 1958, with a couple of friends. While they walked up to the top, I stayed at the bottom looking at the ground. Within a few minutes I had filled a bag with loose potsherds and a dozen broken arrowheads made of obsidian. On the west side of the mound, the side that is swept by the prevailing wind, I could see traces of burnt walls, forming a rectangular pattern. It could mean only one thing—there were many houses. There was no doubt in my mind that these lowest levels were Neolithic; and when my friends reported that they had found Neolithic remains at the top as well, I realised that Çatal Hüyük was all one huge Neolithic city.

I started excavations there in 1961. In spite of the fact that we have so far only managed to conduct four seasons of excavations at Çatal Hüyük, it has yielded such an unparalleled richness of remains that it is a prime example for the study of the Neolithic period.

Çatal Hüyük lies on the Anatolian plateau about fifty kilometres

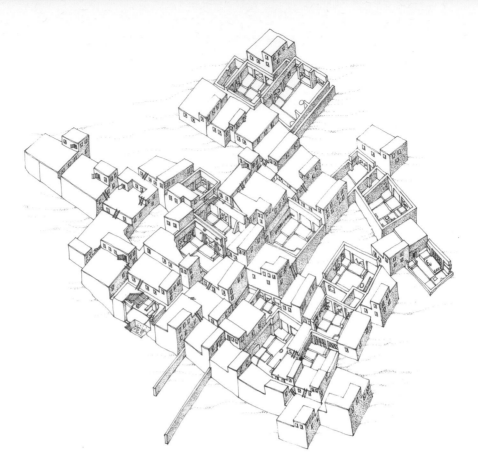

Çatal Hüyük VII:
reconstruction of the
excavated area with
houses and shrines.

south-east of the town of Konya. It is a huge mound covering thirty-two acres, some 600 metres long and about 350 metres wide, and it rises to a height of seventeen metres above the surface of the alluvial plain. We know that it descends at least another five metres below surface level, but the earliest deposits have not yet been excavated and virgin soil has not been reached.

It is one of the largest Neolithic sites known in the Near East, and fourteen successive building-levels have been excavated so far. These levels were dated at the time by the radiocarbon process to 6250–5400 BC; but because of the recent new developments in tree-ring dating, these dates have to be adjusted and are likely to be a full thousand years earlier, say *c*. 7100–6300 BC.

The setting of the site is interesting. It lies on a river that flows from the Taurus Mountains into the Konya Plain, which until 16,000 BC was covered by a huge but shallow lake. Çatal Hüyük was located where two environments met: the grassland with its herds of cattle on the heavy clays of former backswamps, and the well-watered and fertile alluvial wheat-fields. Pastureland and marshes spread to the west and east, and to the north lay bleak salty marshes, the haunts of onagers, wild asses, gazelles and lions. Farther south and west of the site lay the forested ranges of the Taurus Mountains, the 'bull' mountains, inhabited by red, fallow and roe deer and their enemy, the Anatolian leopard, as well as occasional bears. From here the inhabitants of Çatal Hüyük obtained timber for their houses: Scots pine, oak, and juniper. The gallery forest along the river yielded poplar, willow and reeds, and sheltered wild boar, snakes and rats, as well as migrating birds.

Today the whole area, though devoid of trees, is under cultivation, but the site itself is deserted. 9,000 years ago, a visitor to Çatal Hüyük would have been faced with a line of blank walls, a rabbit-warren of flat-topped two-storeyed houses without doors, whose only way of entrance was down a ladder from the roof. It was a huge place—more than a thousand houses, with a population of some 5–6,000 people, at least four times larger than Neolithic Jericho which, until then, could claim to be the largest and oldest city in the world.

Only a small section of the mound has been excavated yet, like a cake with a slice out of it—about three to four per cent of the whole area. But even that small section has been sufficient to give us an extraordinarily vivid and detailed picture of the earliest inhabitants of Çatal Hüyük—where they came from, how they lived and what they lived on, how they died, what they believed in and worshipped, their economy, their religion, their technology, their art. Çatal Hüyük represents the earliest cradle of civilisation we know of—the earliest establishment of the fundamental functions of organised town life, with all manner of world 'firsts' to its credit—the first mirrors, the first pottery, the first textiles, the first wooden vessels, the first paintings on plastered walls. This city lasted for nearly a thousand years until, for some reason not yet clear to us, it was abandoned and rebuilt on the other side of the river.

The economy of the city was based on advanced agriculture, stock-breeding, hunting, and trade; abundance of food enabled specialist craftsmen to develop their arts and technology to an unprecedented level of sophistication. In the plain around Çatal Hüyük, farmers harvested fields irrigated by simple channels. The principal crops were three forms of wheat (emmer, einkorn, and the more advanced hybrid bread wheat), two forms of barley (naked six-row barley and two-row barley), two sorts of peas, lentils, bitter vetch and vetchling, and crucifers grown for the vegetable oil in their seeds. They also cultivated pulses, rich in protein. From the surrounding hills they gathered pistachio nuts and acorns and almonds, hackberry and

Male burial with a pile of arrow-heads, Çatal Hüyük.

juniper berries and crab apples, and they probably grew walnuts and grapes in orchards.

They had domesticated cattle and (later) sheep and goats, and beef seems to have provided nine-tenths of their meat consumption. But hunting had its importance still; they caught and ate giant wild cattle (aurochs), wild sheep, onagers, half-asses, deer of all kinds, wild goats, wild boar, bears, hares and various birds, such as the black crane; they collected birds' eggs, and also did a little fishing. Altogether, it formed the most varied and best-balanced diet known from any Near Eastern Neolithic site—and it showed in the excellent condition of the teeth of the dead we found in the graves. From the skeletons, we can tell much about what the people of Çatal Hüyük were like in life. When people died, their bodies were exposed (probably in a mortuary) until the bones had been picked clean by vultures (wall-paintings depict scenes of giant birds pecking at headless corpses), and then the skeletons, often with their skulls painted and decorated, were buried under the sleeping-platforms in houses. Hundreds of skeletons have been found; and as the houses were frequently rebuilt one on top of the other, several generations of the same family can be studied.

15

OPPOSITE
*Above* View of the alluvial Konya Plain with Mount Karadağ in the centre.

*Below* View of Çatal Hüyük seen from the west across the dried-up riverbed.

About sixty per cent of the population was of the sturdy and robust Eurafrican or Proto-Mediterranean group, with dolichocephalic (long-headed) skulls like their Upper Palaeolithic ancestors. But there were two other racial types present, more recent offshoots of the Eurafricans: the slender, fine-boned Mediterraneans (17%) and the somewhat more numerous round-headed Alpines (24%), both of which had started to appear in the Natufian culture of the Levant around 10,000 BC. This racial diversity must have contributed greatly to the extraordinary vitality of the Çatal Hüyük people. Their average stature was high—170 cm (5 ft 9 ins) for men, 156 cm (5 ft 1½ ins) for women, taller than the average Natufians. Their life-expectancy was greater too: 34·3 years for males, 29·8 for females. Fertility rates were high: the average was 4·2 children per woman, and with an infant mortality rate of 1·8, this would have led to a steady population expansion. In fact, there must have been a constant stream of emigration, and this would explain the rapid spread of Neolithic culture through southern and western Anatolia, for the emigrants would take with them their technology, art, language and beliefs.

This population explosion occurred in the face of several health hazards like endemic malaria, arthritis, and malnutrition, which manifests itself in the hyperostosis of many skulls (a thickening of the blood-carrying vessels of the cranium due to anaemia). Abrasions on the bones show that these people did a lot of running, and broken bones were frequent—not surprisingly, perhaps, when the only entry into their houses was by a ladder from the roof. Head wounds were extremely common, which suggests that there was a lot of quarrelling, as one might expect from a vigorous people living in such a closely cooped-up society. Finally, there was one character who had clearly been gored by a bull, judging by the marks on his pelvis; it was a hazard to be risked by the men who first domesticated that ferocious giant, the auroch—one bull's horn we found there would have measured two metres in length!

We can also tell the sort of clothes they wore, because from carbonised burials we have evidence of the world's first textiles. Their garments were made of plant fibre (not linen), or of a mixture of wool and animal hair, skilfully woven on upright looms. They also used felt, furs, and animal skins. Women's garments were fixed at the shoulder by pins, but male garments had antler toggles and bone belt-hooks and eyes. Ornamental beads were strung on red thread. And, for ceremonial occasions, leopard skins were worn.

The architecture of Çatal Hüyük, the houses and shrines of the

people, is fascinating. There is a remarkable continuity through the fourteen building-levels so far explored, and no sign of any cultural break or hiatus in the sequence. Over a period of nearly a thousand years, Çatal Hüyük was never conquered, although destructive fires occurred from time to time, and such a stretch of peace and prosperity is hard to parallel in later periods of history.

There were no streets as we know them. Each house consisted of a rectangular room, about 25 square metres in area, with a narrow storeroom added along one side, built of proper mud-brick and plaster without stone foundations. There were no 'party walls'; each house had its own walls, and the houses were grouped in extensive blocks next to each other and entered only from the roof. Each house had a partial upper storey built of wood and plaster. The blocks of houses were separated by occasional courtyards which served as dumping grounds for domestic rubbish, and for outdoor sanitation. The city had no walls or special fortification; the outside of the settlement was formed by a blank wall without entry, with cattle pens stuck on to it—the prototype for the casemate wall. Wooden ladders fixed against the south wall of each main room led into the buildings, which were lit by small apertures set below the eaves of the flat roofs in at least two of the walls.

The interior of each building was broadly similar. Along the south end of the room was the entrance ladder and the kitchen quarter with a hearth, oven and fuel cupboard. Two wooden posts along the east wall carried the two roof beams and the flat roof. Against the east wall there was a large platform for the woman of the house, with a bench extending from it; in the north-east corner there was a smaller platform for the man of the house, and there were subsidiary ones for the children and any relatives who might be staying. These platforms served as sofas for sitting and sleeping, and it was underneath them that the dead were buried. The walls were panelled and plastered afresh every year, and some panels were decorated with simple red paint.

The artefacts found in these houses are of special interest because we can trace through them the development of their technology. Pottery, for instance, was used throughout the entire occupation of the site, though on a limited scale at first. From Level XIII onwards, a cream-burnished heavy straw-tempered ware appears, with simple bowl and hole-mouth shapes. From Level VIII we find a thinner dark burnished ware, grit-tempered, and used mainly as kitchen ware for cooking. The development continued, and pottery became more

17

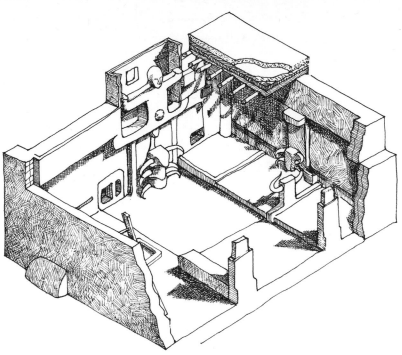

Shrine from Çatal Hüyük VI showing relief of a goddess in position of childbirth to ram's head over a framework with superimposed bull's heads.

frequently used. By Level III, the first attempts were being made to decorate cream-coloured pottery with smears of paint.

We can also trace the development of basketry and wooden vessels. Wood was used for making large dishes, bowls of various sorts, cups and boxes fitted with lids. In basketry, cereal straw and marsh grass were used for making twilled floor-mats, and coiled baskets fitted with lids. Bone was used for making awls, needles, spoons, scoops, polishers and handles for various implements.

Tools and weapons were made of obsidian and flint, and showed a great diversity of range. Flint had to be imported from north Syria, and was only used for special implements like ceremonial daggers. Obsidian (a black volcanic rock like bottle-glass) was widely used for arrow-heads, spear-heads, and blades of all kinds, including sickles; and from some of the women's graves came obsidian mirrors, the earliest known in the world, which may have been used not only for cosmetic purposes but for magical rituals and divination. Grave-goods were found in a number of graves, but by no means all; some men would be buried with their weapons, women with their jewellery, and some of the more important male burials had polished stone mace-heads as well.

Apart from the developments in pottery and textiles, there is evidence for early metallurgy at Çatal Hüyük; the use of lead and copper, both native and smelted, for trinkets, tubes, beads, and perhaps for awls and drills.

The many raw materials found on the site attest to a widespread system of exchange and barter, for in the alluvial plain itself only clay, wood, reeds and bone were to be found near the settlement. All other materials were brought in from near or far, and a fascinating network of trade-routes can be drawn linking many of the satellite settlements with Çatal Hüyük throughout the Konya Plain and beyond. Among the exotic imports were Mediterranean shells such as dentalium, whelks and cockles, tabular flint from Syria, cowrie shells from the Red Sea, raw copper (possibly from Ergani across the Euphrates), lead from the lead mines near the Cilician Gates, turquoise-like apatite from central Anatolia, and much else. From nearer at hand came minerals like ground malachite and azurite, haematite, limonite, red ochre and cinnabar for use as paints, greenstone for the manufacture of axes, adzes, chisels and other carpenters' tools, volcanic stone for querns and mortars, white marble, and limestone. The general picture is one of a highly organised trading system, in which distance and expense seemed no obstacle.

European archaeologists frequently talk about archaeology as the recovery of rubbish, and they stress that archaeology hardly ever yields evidence of man's thought. But here Çatal Hüyük is different, and that is because many of the one-roomed houses clearly served a special purpose as shrines. They are distinguished from ordinary houses by their religious decoration, by the presence of cult statues and statuettes, and by richer burials with ceremonial weapons; each one seems to have been the cult place for three or four of the surrounding houses.

Shrine from Çatal Hüyük VI with plaster relief showing double-headed and double-bodied figure giving birth to small and large bull's head.

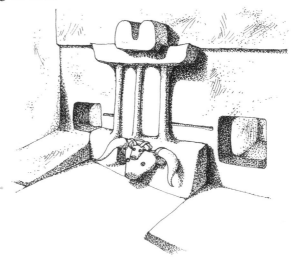

The interpretation of the material in these shrines is necessarily subjective, demanding skills with which not every archaeologist is equipped. First of all we have the cult objects themselves : these are divided into well-modelled statuettes and crude figurines. The first are interpreted as cult statues, usually found in groups, whereas the figurines (both human and animal) were used as votive offerings (*ex votos*) and were not part of the permanent cult inventory.

Among the statuettes, women predominate, and men are much less common; various ages are represented, from young girl to old crone and from young boy to bearded man. Associations with animals such as bulls and leopards and birds of prey occur, and the common presence of stalactites and accretions with the cult statues may suggest a chthonic (cavelike) setting, like a Christmas crib. One unusual group shows two women in one — both aspects of the goddess, virgin and mother, the ancestor of the two-headed female pots and figurines of later times. Another small slab has an embracing couple on the left and a mother and child on the right — a narrative in stone of the birth of the young god, whose birth is also shown in a large clay figure of a birth-giving goddess supported by lions.

In the shrines there are two types of relief: modelled high relief, permanently visible even when whitewashed, and cut-out silhouettes of animals or animal heads, which damage the plaster of the walls and are always the final type of decoration found in a shrine. The bold reliefs include female figures, usually with uplifted arms and legs (a posture of childbirth), or with arms outstretched as if dancing or whirling. Male figures are not found, but their place is taken by bull's heads, or more rarely stag's and ram's heads, with horn cores or antlers incorporated into the modelled plaster. The only animal fully portrayed is the leopard, single or paired, a symbol of the goddess.

Some of the composite reliefs are of monumental size, sometimes higher than the adjacent walls, suggesting that a section of the roof had to be raised to accommodate them; they can be as high as 4·5 metres. A number of goddesses are shown giving birth to horned animal heads, symbolising male offspring. Other symbolic scenes show women's breasts modelled on the tusked lower jaws of wild boars, or full pendant breasts containing the skulls of scavengers such as griffon vultures, weasels, or foxes. Death in the midst of life?

The wall paintings show great variety, from simple red panels to elaborate polychrome paintings covering whole shrines. Sometimes they imitate gaily patterned textiles or cut-out felt patterns, others show nets or form a composition of human hands. There is a picture of an erupting volcano with a town in the foreground. Several of the pictures are connected with death—giant vultures pecking at headless corpses, or a man armed with a sling driving vultures from a corpse, or a man carrying blood-smeared human heads. One picture shows a strange mortuary building made of reeds and matting, with human skulls and parts of bodies below it. A few scenes show deer hunts, but two whole shrines show festivities—animal games in which armed men sport with a variety of creatures, bulls, wild deer, wild boars, bears, lions, and so on; they are baiting them by pulling their tails and tongues, or attempting to capture them, but without any signs of doing violence to the animal. Could these be ceremonies relating to animal domestication—or are they pictorial records of myths and legends without which no religion is complete? Certain enigmatic scenes would favour the latter interpretation. But a great deal more work has to be done at Çatal Hüyük before we can ever hope to give answers to the many questions raised by its discovery—a discovery that holds the key, or a key at least, to the origins of Near Eastern civilisation.

Obviously, the Neolithic 'civilisation' of Çatal Hüyük did not come into being overnight, but represents a climax of a process that must

White marble figure of double goddess from Çatal Hüyük VI.

ÇATAL HÜYÜK: THE NEOLITHIC REVOLUTION

have started in the Upper Palaeolithic *c*. 35,000–10,000 BC.* Several features at Çatal Hüyük show links with the distant past: the physical anthropology of the bulk of the population, the habit of burying skeletons smeared with red ochre, and the decorative paintings of the shrines with the use of broken-off stalactites in the cult, reminiscent of earlier cave sanctuaries.

More immediately, a handful of sites from the eighth millennium, a thousand years before Çatal Hüyük, have yielded limited evidence of the existence of small agricultural settlements which grew crops, gathered fruits, and hunted wild animals. It is possible that the domestication of animals started during this period, because by 7000 BC fully domesticated cattle, sheep, goats, pigs and dogs were arriving by sea at Knossos in Crete (where they were not native), almost certainly from Anatolia. These early Anatolian farmers lived in rectangular mud-brick rooms in permanent settlements, plastered and often painted. The striking feature about the few sites that have been excavated, however, is that they are all different; it is not until the Çatal Hüyük period that some uniformity of culture appears.

At present, these can only be tentative conclusions. The origins of this Neolithic civilisation are still very obscure. The study of the pre-pottery period in Anatolia can hardly be said to have begun; we are still groping in the dark.

*The period in which Modern man (Homo sapiens sapiens) first appeared — best known for its so-called 'cave art' of France, Spain and Italy.

# 2

# Hacılar: Early Painted Pottery

Around 6300 BC the site of Çatal Hüyük was moved across the river, for some reason still unknown to us, and rebuilt as Çatal Hüyük West. And at about the same time, there is evidence of destruction at a Late Neolithic site some 300 kilometres further west, at Hacılar.

The following period, 6300–5650 BC, is known as the Early Chalcolithic period—literally, 'Copper-Stone', for it is during this period that copper tools begin to supersede stone tools. The main sites associated with this period are Mersin in Cilicia (excavated by John Garstang), Can Hasan (excavated by David French), Erbaba (excavated by Jacques Bordaz), Çatal Hüyük West (still largely unexcavated) and Hacılar, which I excavated in four seasons starting in 1958. Of these sites, it is Hacılar that has produced the most spectacular examples of the chief innovation that is the hallmark of this period—the development of painted pottery.

Despite the upheaval at Hacılar and Çatal Hüyük, there is no evidence to suggest that the new culture was introduced from elsewhere; on the contrary, all the evidence points to a strong continuity of tradition, with local developments of varying degree.

In the Late Neolithic settlement at Hacılar (Level VI), the architecture was different from that at Çatal Hüyük in one salient respect: houses were no longer entered through the roof. Each house opened directly onto an open courtyard by means of wide double doors. Narrow alleyways made their appearance for the first time.

There were developments in the basic economy, too. Improvements in irrigation and animal husbandry led to a decline in hunting and with it of the fine obsidian industry; arrow-heads and spear-heads were replaced by the mace and the sling. The decline in

23

Baked clay statuette of
mother and child.
The child's head is
restored.

the chipped-stone industry was probably hastened by the growing use
of copper, although no traces of metal have yet been found in the
earliest layers of the period. One side-effect of this technological
progress was a marked deterioration in the condition of the people's
teeth, as gritty cereal foods took the place of a more balanced diet.

These developments were reflected in art, too. With the end of
hunting, major wall-paintings disappeared; the status of man
dwindled with it, and males were no longer represented in their own
right, while there was an increase in the representation of female
deities with exaggerated hips and buttocks. Elaborately decorated
shrines gave way to domestic cults, and statuettes appeared in every
house, as if religion had become a more private affair.

The dead were now buried outside the settlement in cemeteries and
not inside the houses. These cemeteries have not yet been
systematically excavated, but pottery vessels were buried with the
dead for the first time, and in the latest phase at Hacılar
anthropomorphic vessels and clay statuettes have turned up,
reputedly found in many graves.

Religious imagery at Hacılar developed strongly along earlier lines,
with goddesses associated with children or leopards, rare male deities,
double figures of goddesses, and painted figures of various animals
and birds, including exotic beasts.

But the major feature of the period was the growing dominance of
clay over stone. Clay statuettes soon outnumbered their counterparts
in stone, and the artists working in clay developed an excellence that
was hardly ever surpassed in later periods. Pottery rather than
plastered walls became the major medium for painted decoration.
The innovations were fascinating: geometric designs based on textile
and basketry patterns dominated in the Konya Plain, while further
to the west, the more conservative artists of Hacılar retained and
modified the old symbolic representations for much longer.

It was not that the vitality of the Neolithic period had withered in
its descendants, but that it was channelled into what is frequently
called the minor arts—pottery and textiles, which lacked monumental quality but were as fine as, if not finer than, anything that had been
produced in the past. The Early Chalcolithic pottery of Hacılar
marked an unsurpassed height of achievement in the boldness and
elegance of its shapes and patterns.

Near the end of the Early Chalcolithic period, the settlement at
Hacılar was destroyed by fire (Level II), probably by enemy action.
Instead of building on the burnt ruins of the previous settlement, the

newcomers at Hacılar built a huge fortress around the ancient mound, 150 metres in diameter. Encircling a large open space, the rooms of this fortress had excessively thick walls, and once again access could only be gained through the roof. Even so, this fortress was razed by some unknown enemy around 5650 BC, at about the same time as Mersin and Can Hasan were also burnt. Hacılar was now abandoned for ever, apart from some squatter occupation, although both Mersin and Can Hasan continued to be occupied and provided cultural continuity into a Middle Chalcolithic period (5650–5000 BC); this was characterised by fine pottery painted in more than one colour, a climax of the south Anatolian ceramic tradition. The first bronze tools made of copper with a small admixture of tin appeared in Mersin around 5200 BC; at the same time there was a marked decline in the production of pottery statuettes and figurines. This phenomenon is hard to explain unless the more widespread use of metal was responsible; it is possible that sheet-metal figurines were now being made, as in the Balkans, but no cemeteries have yet been found from this period which might supply the answer.

The Late Chalcolithic period of Anatolia (5500 or 5000 to 4000 BC) is still very much a Dark Age as far as we are concerned; but it represented a very distinct break. Historically speaking the end of the Hacılar culture was probably produced by a movement of 'barbarians' from north-western Anatolia, beyond the zone of the painted pottery cultures, who now took over in the south and imposed an inferior pottery culture of their own which showed little sign of further development during its long existence.

Hacılar I anthropomorphic pot.

The type-site for this period is Beycesultan, 200 kilometres north-west of Hacılar, which was excavated by Seton Lloyd and myself from 1954 to 1959. At Beycesultan, the newcomers settled on virgin soil, and left us a unique uninterrupted sequence of more than twenty building-levels, forming a mound eleven metres high by the end of the period.

They were a settled people, not nomads, and practised agriculture and stockbreeding, and they spun and wove woollen cloth like their predecessors. But one highly significant development was reflected in the discovery of a small hoard of copper objects at an early level. It was a collection of fifteen objects in a pot, and it included a fragment of a dagger, a chisel, two awls, three needles, and some fragments in hammered copper as well as a silver ring. It showed that this once precious metal, copper, was becoming more plentiful and was now in ordinary household use.

Houses of rectangular oblong plan were neatly built of mud-brick and plaster, and consisted of a single room, sometimes entered from a porch on the narrow side leading from a court or alley. They contained hearths and storage bins, and occasionally benches and platforms. Party walls were not uncommon, and the roofs were probably flat.

Infants were buried in coarse pots below the floor, but adults must have been buried outside the settlement in cemeteries. Evidence of religious practices is scanty, and we have no shrines and very few figurines, but late in the period a very distinctive type of marble figurine appeared, with a stylised body and a circular head tilted backwards.

The most abundant material from the excavation is, of course, the pottery, which occurred in two variants: a coarse reddish ware which was used for storage vessels, cooking and burial, and a fine burnished and slipped straw-tempered ware in a variety of dark colours. One innovation of the period is jugs with handles, frequently horned handles imitating stylised animals or animal heads. The contrast between this new and heavy pottery with the elegant painted pottery of Hacılar is most marked, and leaves no doubt that the two traditions were quite unrelated.

But however drab the Late Chalcolithic cultures may seem to us in comparison (chiefly in the light of insufficient knowledge and inadequate excavation), their importance should not be under-estimated, for it would appear that they were ancestral to the various Bronze Age cultures of Anatolia. Only large-scale area excavations of settlement sites and cemeteries will enable us to assess them in proper perspective.

# 3

# Troy and Alaca Höyük: the Early Bronze Age

Until recently, the dividing line between the Late Chalcolithic period and Early Bronze Age in Anatolia was drawn at a date of *c.* 3100 BC, in line with the establishment of the First Dynasty in Egypt. This was the first absolute historical date in the ancient Near East, and the development of other cultures in the Near East and the Aegean were all correlated to it. In the absence of other absolute evidence, everything hinged on that one date, 3100 BC, when the unification of Upper and Lower Egypt took place.

With the introduction of 'calibrated' radiocarbon dating (C14 dates corrected by tree-ring dates), the picture has altered considerably, and the dates of other cultures like Egypt have been put back by up to 300 years — back to about 3400 BC. Moreover, carbon dating has greatly helped in correlating widely separated cultures from the Aegean to Turkestan and India which were archaeologically related by an ever-increasing trade in raw materials such as copper and tin, and semi-precious stones like lapis lazuli, cornelian, agate, and so on.

Yet this is only part of the story, for archaeological research shows that this culmination of civilisation, represented in Egypt by the unification of the two kingdoms, had a long earlier history. In Mesopotamia, a period of intensified economic growth coincided with the development of the earliest writings found at Uruk (Biblical Erech, modern Warka), the earliest of the great city-states of Sumer. In spite of dynastic breaks, cultural development was continuous, and there is no justification for suggesting that there was a sharp break anywhere.

In Anatolian archaeology this had been recognised for some time, and the Early Bronze Age label now includes its ancestral phase, taking us back to *c.* 4000 BC as marking the boundary between Chalcolithic and 'EBA', as it is usually written in archaeological textbooks. And, in fact, around this time there was a marked change in culture throughout many other parts of the Near East as well, in Egypt, Mesopotamia and Palestine.

Evidence is steadily accumulating in the Fertile Crescent to suggest that during the fifth millennium BC important changes in social structure were taking place connected with the growth of population, the accumulation of greater food production through irrigation, and the need for stricter political control. In Sumer (Lower Mesopotamia) and Elam (south-western Iran), this soon led to the development of early states with priest-kings with considerable power. It was a gradual process, but within a few hundred years vast complexes of mud-brick temples were appearing at Uruk and other early Sumerian cities, soon to be followed by the invention of writing to record the new-found wealth, and the use of cylinder seals to identify the tribute and merchandise that was flowing into these early cities from abroad, through trading-posts especially established for that purpose. The two main cities engaged in these commercial enterprises were Uruk in the heart of Sumer, and Susa, the capital of Elam; and there is widespread archaeological evidence for the way in which the trade routes they controlled covered huge areas of the Near and Middle East.

This growing interest in mercantile activity, evidently encouraged by mutual interest and effected through treaties and messengers (the early Sumerian texts have words for both 'merchant' and 'herald') led to a breakdown of the former isolation and marks the beginning of a new era: the Early Bronze Age. Not all contact was peaceful, though; early seals show the king smiting his enemies, leading troops, and besieging cities. Kingship was developing fast, and increasingly larger territorial units were coming into being through conquest—best exemplified by the first historical records of the conquest of Lower Egypt by King Narmer of Upper Egypt, the celebrated unification of Egypt that gave rise to the First Dynasty in *c.* 3400 BC. Egypt broke free from its bonds of African isolation and started trade expansion of its own. Parallel to Sumer and Elam, Egypt also (and probably quite independently) had been developing writing for the same administrative purposes, but as the Egyptians wrote on papyrus, which has not survived, only labels of wood, bone and ivory, or cursive inscriptions on pots, occur beside a few hieroglyphs on ceremonial and royal objects of stone—the first historical records in the world.

In marked contrast to its southern neighbours, none of the Early Bronze Age cultures of Anatolia has yet yielded any evidence for writing, except at the very end of the period—although it should be said that none of these cultures has been investigated on the sort of scale that would definitely rule out the use of writing. In the absence of written texts, we know nothing of the kind of political organisation of Anatolia at this time, but on the evidence of later references it seems likely that the usual form of government was city-states rather than large kingdoms, although this does not rule out the possibility of temporary hegemonies of one state over many others, as in Mesopotamia, or of loose confederations. Historically speaking, the Early Bronze Age of Anatolia still belongs to prehistory.

Although the archaeological evidence remains scanty, it is reasonable to assume from what evidence there is that Anatolia had vigorous and widespread trade contacts with Mesopotamia, and that they were largely responsible for the initiation of the Bronze Age in Turkey. The ultimate stimulus was the need of Mesopotamia and Syria, and to a lesser degree Egypt, for raw materials: timber, and especially metals, of which Anatolia had more than anyone else, apart from tin. The development of metallurgy in Anatolia put her ahead of all her neighbours, and though the exact processes are by no means as straightforward or simple as many archaeologists have imagined, it was the key to the development of Bronze Age civilisations in Turkey. It was a very gradual affair, as might be imagined, and there is little metal in circulation at the beginning of the Bronze Age (EB1, 'Early Bronze Age 1', c. 4000–3400 BC). It is not until EB2 (c. 3400–2700 BC) that we find more, with copper, arsenical copper and tin-bronze all occurring side by side; but the climax of metalworking, not only of copper, arsenical copper or tin bronze, but also of gold, electrum, silver, and some occasional iron, is the EB3 period c. 2700–2150 BC. The term Early Bronze Age is therefore clearly a misnomer.

Yet, though archaeologists complain about the lack of direct evidence, there is indirect evidence to help us fill in the picture of early metallurgy. In the first place, there is an almost total absence of stone-cutting tools in EBA deposits, which suggests that stone implements were not widely used and that metal was far more common than the few finds would seem to indicate. Secondly, there is the unmistakable influence of metal prototypes for much of the pottery, with its shining burnished surfaces, its metallic handles, shapes, carinations, spouts, rivets and grooves and so on. Unlike pottery, however, which was simply discarded when it was broken, metal was too precious to throw away; it was remelted over and over again, and only if metal objects were buried with the dead, or lost in burnt buildings which were abandoned, will the archaeologist find them, unless he stumbles across a metalworker's shop or a metal-worker's hoard, both of which are extremely rare finds. Our direct evidence is therefore very limited; but here again the excellence of Anatolian metalwork and its early technical sophistication give clear indications of long practice and experience which must be projected backwards in time, and help to bridge the gaps between isolated finds of objects and weapons.

The study of metal prospecting, extraction and smelting in Anatolia has only just started, and it would appear that most of the work was carried out on a small scale by the smiths near the sources in the mountains, wherever timber was easily available. The actual hammering and casting of objects may have been done near the source, or perhaps from ingots in workshops in the cities or the palace, because broken moulds are common in settlement sites. The question of whether smiths were itinerant or resident cannot be decided at present—perhaps both kinds existed.

Metallurgy and trade were two important features of the EBA economy of Turkey; but the basis of the economy, as before, was agriculture and stock-breeding. Unfortunately, this is a subject that has been much neglected in Anatolian archaeology, and we lack many details. Generally the same crops were grown as before: wheat and barley, peas and lentils and bitter vetch, either by dry farming or with irrigation. Grapes, figs and olives were certainly grown in appropriate surroundings; the Anatolians were clearly fond of wine, for in nearly every grave the dead person was supplied with beak-spouted jugs and cups. Oil lamps also first made their appearance in EBA. Teapots, some with strainers, began to appear around 2500 BC, suggesting that brewed beverages made from herbs were becoming popular; and coarse drinks like beer may have been consumed from mugs and the peculiar two-handled goblets known as *depas*—they were probably two-handled so that they could be passed on to a neighbour at drinking parties. There is very little evidence for hunting, and EBA arrow-heads are almost unknown, yet it is unlikely that hunting, fishing and fowling did not take place, and there are other ways of catching one's prey that leave no archaeological record, such as netting. Domestic animals included cattle, sheep, goats, pigs, and probably donkeys, while pot shapes suggest the presence of

The various building
levels of Poliochni.
(*Roman numbers in
key for building
levels*).

POLIOCHNI

| EB III | ■ | V |
| EB II | ▨ | IV |
| EB II | ▦ | III |
| EB I | ☐ | II |

0    10    20    30    40 M.

OPPOSITE
*Above* View of the old excavations of Troy.

*Below* The fortress of Van, the ancient Urartian capital.

domesticated geese and ducks. Only the horse was still unknown.

Decorated spindle whorls are exceedingly common on EBA sites, indicating that weaving was widely practised. Loom-weights are equally common, although only a few impressions of textiles have been found. However, incised patterns and painted designs on pottery are very like those on modern Turkish textiles, and this suggests that patterned or embroidered fabrics were made.

Throughout the long EBA period in Anatolia, inhumation (simple flexed or extended burial) was the rule, either in pot (pithos) burials large enough to hold several or successive family burials, or in individual graves lined with bricks, stones (cists) or wood, or just dug into the earth. Rock-cut tombs as found in the Aegean or Palestine at this time do not apparently occur; and cremation, although known in North Syria during EB3, was still unknown in Anatolia. With the exception of a few princely burials, funeral gifts are distinguished by their parsimony: a few pots and a dagger or knife for males, a few items of jewellery for a woman, and perhaps a flat marble idol with a child burial. Infants were frequently buried in the house, and intramural burial of adults is found in central and eastern Anatolia, but never in such quantities as to suggest that everybody was buried there; hence, extramural cemeteries must have existed as well. In western Anatolia, burial in extramural cemeteries was the rule.

However, one must always be careful about making wide generalisations. Turkey showed not one uniform culture but a mass of distinct culture provinces, many of which can easily be subdivided into smaller areas. Many had fluctuating boundaries, varying from period to period, yet, based on the physical geography of the country, most of these areas preserved their identity through the ages and they are just as apparent today as in the Bronze Age. We must not forget that the Early Bronze Age covered a period of nearly two thousand years—equivalent in time, say, from the birth of Christ to the beginning of the reign of Queen Victoria; and that in area, if Anatolia were superimposed on a modern map of Europe, it would stretch from the Straits of Dover to the Russian frontier.

We still know very little about the architecture of the Early Bronze Age. The main site to have yielded impressive remains from EB1 is the Anatolian settlement at Poliochni, on the island of Lemnos in the northern Aegean, which was excavated by an Italian expedition in the 1930s and subsequently published after stratigraphic checks by Bernabo Brea.

Poliochni was founded in EB1, and was considerably older than

Troy. It was a city some 250 metres long, surrounded by a stone fortification wall with towers flanking a narrow gate. Just within the gate lay two public buildings, a long and narrow granary and a large open building with two-tiered benches along one of the long sides. The houses were of the so-called megaron type—long houses with a hall and a porch on the narrow side through which the building was entered, to which other subsidiary rooms may have been attached.

With the passage of time, Poliochni expanded outside the original city walls, and new fortifications with gates and formidable buttresses were built at the start of EB2. By EB3 (2700–2150 BC) a clear system of town planning was apparent, with main roads and side-streets branching off at approximately right angles in a grid pattern. Each of the blocks of houses contained at least one megaron, sometimes two, with enclosed courtyards and at least one row of subsidiary rooms on the long side of the building. Two small town squares have been found, each with a well; one of the squares had a free-standing megaron and a room without a door in which two bodies were found—the result of some disaster, apparently an earthquake, that overwhelmed the city. It has been surmised that this megaron, with its central placing, was a public building, perhaps a courthouse with a prison next door.

What was striking about Poliochni was the absence of a palace or temple, but it should be remembered that a large part of the site, facing the harbour, was eroded by the sea, and the main buildings may well have been along the waterfront. Without the public buildings, our picture of an early Anatolian EBA city is incomplete; but we can complete the picture with the temples excavated at Beycesultan in south-west Anatolia.

The earliest temple at Beycesultan dated from the late EB1. It was built roughly in the megaron form: the house of the deity is frequently similar to the house of the worshipper, though often grander and provided with features such as altars, 'horns of consecration', and the screens deemed necessary for the cult and therefore absent in normal dwellings. In later levels at Beycesultan two temples were found, with features suggesting a pair of sanctuaries.

The most celebrated city-site in Anatolia is the small mound of Hisarlik, overlooking the Dardanelles, which is usually equated with the classical Homeric site of Troy. It was identified as such in 1871 by the German 'archaeologist' Heinrich Schliemann, who excavated it in seven major campaigns in the 1870s and 1880s, in the course of which he convinced himself that he had found Homeric Troy and even the

33

'Treasure of King Priam'. Fresh excavations were carried out in the 1930s by an American expedition from the University of Cincinnati led by Carl Blegen, which redefined the stratigraphy and corrected Schliemann's chronology of the site. Although Blegen fully accepted the identification of Hisarlik with Homeric Troy, the equation, however, remains unproved; it rests on the circumstantial premise that *if* there ever had been a Troy in the region where Homer and Greek tradition said there was, then it could only have stood on the site of Hisarlik, strategically placed to dominate sea and land trade routes at the Dardanelles.

The First Settlement of Troy (Troy I) was a small village, about 100 metres in diameter. It seems to have been founded in EB2 (3400–2700 BC), but a recent reappraisal of the evidence suggests that it was not until around 3250 BC, a century or so before the end of Troy I, that it was surrounded by a massive stone wall with entrances flanked by towers. This was nearly a thousand years after Poliochni had become a fortified city. Little remains of what lay inside the walls; there seems to have been a small number of relatively large free-standing houses, but there was at least one big megaron accompanied

Tentative reconstruction of male and female cult figures, horns of consecration and ritual circles and offerings in shrine of Beycesultan XIV, (EB2).

Sophia Schliemann wearing gold ornaments from the last phase of Troy II.

by further buildings, and this complex has been interpreted as a palace, or at least the residence of a ruler, however petty.

The need for fortifications implies a need for security, and therefore the possession of goods which others might covet. In the case of Troy, these might have been derived from trade; Troy I has yielded some of the earliest tin-bronzes, suggesting that these people had access to a source of tin which many scholars believe may have been in Europe, perhaps in Yugoslavia or farther afield in Bohemia. That contacts with Europe were close is shown by Troy I influence on contemporary pottery in eastern Bulgaria (Thrace), and by similar Trojan ceramics along the northern shore of the Aegean and penetrating up the Vardar River into Macedonia. What is not known is whether this implies influence on local cultures, as in Bulgaria, or actual Trojan settlements established along a trade route into Europe. Nor is it clear whether these influences came from Troy, rather than from the great island site of Poliochni on Lemnos. The fact remains that Troy I culture dominated the northern Aegean.

35

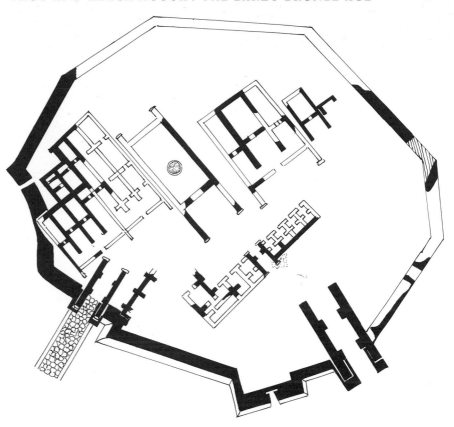

Two phases of the
Troy II fort, IIc and
IIg, Early Bronze Age 2
period.

Troy I was destroyed by a catastrophic fire around 3100 BC. Over the debris a new and larger citadel was built, with no appreciable break in cultural continuity. This Second Settlement, which lasted about 500 years, had at least twelve phases; midway through, one of them was destroyed by fire—Blegen's Troy IIc. Troy at this period contained a huge megaron, about 45 metres long, flanked by two narrower ones facing onto a walled court entered through a gate, with storage rooms (rather than a colonnade) lining the court. Of several other buildings, one is regarded as a 'shrine', on rather insufficient grounds. The whole complex is called a palace; but one could equally well argue that the great megara represented temples, and that the subsidiary buildings were living quarters for 'Trojan kings'. There simply is not enough evidence for sure identification of the function of any buildings at 'Troy'—nor, for that matter, anywhere else in EBA Turkey, as sceptics may point out.

With the destruction of Troy IIc, *c.* 2700 BC, a change into EB3 came over the site, and various further building-levels sheltered within the patched-up walls; the city now consisted of blocks of

houses on a grid pattern like contemporary Poliochni, but with one larger building that may have been a royal residence. The change in architecture was accompanied by the increasing use of the potter's wheel, and wheel-made pottery in plain or red-coated kitchen ware that had first appeared at the beginning of Troy II now took over completely from the burnished grey, brown and red vessels that had been made by hand in the Troy I tradition.

Troy II suffered a catastrophic end around 2550 BC. Every single excavated house showed evidence of hasty and frantic evacuation as a great fire swept through the city. Gold objects and other treasures had been dropped or buried: and it was to this phase of Troy that Schliemann's celebrated 'Treasure of Priam' belonged—a full fifteen hundred years before Priam could have lived if the sack of Troy is traditionally dated to 1196 BC. It was to this final destruction of Troy II that we owe the preservation of the great quantity of precious objects that Schliemann recovered. These 'treasures' afford striking proof of the high level of wealth and artistic sophistication of Troy at this time: vessels of gold and silver and electrum, beautifully carved battle-axes in semi-precious stones such as nephrite and lapis lazuli from Badakshan, carved lion's-head rock-crystal pommels for swords and daggers, silver spear-heads, and a great mass of gold jewellery — diadems, ear-rings (with or without pendants), lock rings, bracelets, and pendants with granulation and filigree work. It is little wonder that Schliemann was overwhelmed by his discovery.

The catastrophe that overtook Troy II was also reflected in a great destruction which my archaeological survey noted at about a hundred city and village sites on the Konya Plain, dated to around 2650 BC. Some scholars have tentatively linked this destruction with the name of the founder of the Akkadian Empire in Mesopotamia around 2445 BC — the great Sargon of Akkad. With Sargon, history and legend are hard to distinguish. Very late sources suggest that he waged military campaigns deep into Asia Minor, as far as the central Anatolian plateau, where he took a city called Puruskhanda (the ancient city of Burushattum) in Cappadocia. His grandson, Naram-Sin, was also reputed to have led an expedition to Puruskhanda, and to have waged war against a coalition of Anatolian kings. Puruskhanda was probably the site known as Acemköy, and only excavation of the deeper levels there could throw light on the reliability of these traditions. At present there is no incontrovertible evidence that either of these powerful Akkadian kings ever extended their sway as far as Cilicia or the Anatolian plateau.

The EB3 period (2700–2150 BC) is no less difficult to elucidate. Troy III and Troy IV were essentially a poor continuation of Late Troy II. In the Konya Plain there are perhaps a dozen large city-sites still unexcavated, a tremendous potential not yet tapped by archaeology. The largest site that has been excavated in Cilicia is Tarsus, later to be the home town of the Apostle Paul. The site of ancient Tarsus was excavated by Hetty Goldman in the 1930s and just after the war. It is small in comparison with the Konya Plain sites, only some 250 metres in diameter. The EB3 layers at this site show a western Anatolian culture with megaron complexes and wheel-made red pottery; but the earlier EB2 remains afforded a fascinating glimpse of city life, as a street with two-storeyed houses on either side, a shop and a tavern with a back-room for drinking were excavated. The houses had elaborate hearths, often with a thronelike seat made of mud-brick next to the hearth; and some of the rooms were so well preserved that doors with lintels were still intact, and niches were set

38

into the walls. In the sweltering heat of the Cilician summer the inhabitants evidently slept on the roofs, as they do today. This city was burnt sometime during EB2, and as a precaution against future disaster the people demolished one half of the street and constructed a city wall with a gate, to which a ramp led up from the plain near the river. We have the entrance to the city but little else, for the excavations were, as so often in the Near East, limited to large soundings.

From the finds it is clear that the people of Tarsus manufactured hand-made pottery but imported wheel-made Syrian ware; they traded with Cyprus and with western Anatolia, and it is probably from here that the idea of wheel-made pottery spread to Troy. A Cilician jug turned up in Egypt, in a grave in the necropolis at Giza dated late in the reign of King Cheops of the Fourth Dynasty (*c*. 2800 BC), the builder of the Great Pyramid. Cilicia had few resources except timber, foodstuffs, and perhaps linen, for flax could be cultivated there. More important, however, was its strategic position on the trade route from the Anatolian plateau to Syria and Mesopotamia—the gold and silver for Sumer probably passed through Cilician hands on its way east.

It is in northern Anatolia that we find the most spectacular EB2 site of all—the thirteen 'Royal Tombs' of Alaca Höyük. It lies near Boğazköy, about 150 kilometres east of Ankara, and the tombs date from the period between 2900 and 2700 BC. They were excavated in the 1930s by Professors Remzi Oğuz Arik and Hamit Zübeyr Kosay.

The tombs were large rectangles lined with wood or stone, some of

Arrangement of body, gifts and pots in royal tomb at Alaca Höyük, with head and leg bones of sacrificed cattle originally placed on the wooden roof.

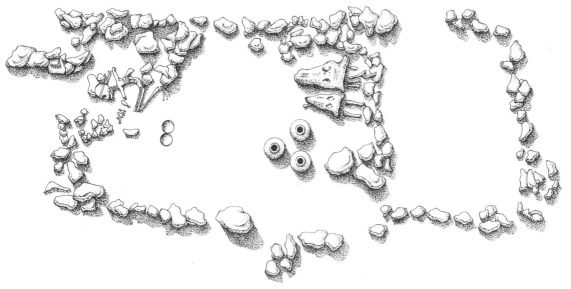

Bronze standard with stag and bulls from Alaca Höyük.

them 6–8 metres long, more like rooms than tombs; they were about a metre deep, roofed with timber and clay. The body was buried in a corner in a contracted position, surrounded by great quantities of funeral gifts: iron daggers (some of the earliest examples of worked iron), bronze spears, gold-mounted maces, battle-axes, small metal figurines, metal vessels, weapons, jewellery and a few pots. The rest of the grave would be empty except for a mysterious 'standard'—on which was mounted a splendid figurine of a deer or a bull, about one foot high, made of bronze inlaid with gold or silver. There were also a varying number of 'sun-discs', a number of 'horns', pointed 'goads', and other enigmatic objects. The remains of a funerary feast were found on the roof: neatly arranged skulls and leg-bones of sacrificial oxen.

There can be no doubt about the importance of this area, politically, artistically and technologically. This was evidently a royal cemetery; there may even be further tombs still to be discovered, for,

40

unbelievable as it may seem, the excavations of the cemetery were not continued. Further investigation is needed, because there is still great uncertainty about their date and about the order in which the tombs followed one another, as they lay on the slope of the mound.

The site of Alaca Höyük is most probably the holy city of Arinna, the prime cult centre of the Sun-goddess of Arinna, the wife of the Weather-god of Hatti, the chief deity of central Anatolia in the second and probably also the third millennium BC. Hattus, the capital of Hatti, later to become the Hittite capital of Hattusa (modern Boğazköy), was only fifty kilometres away. Tawiniya (modern Eskiyapan?), another important site, lay between the two; it is now being excavated by Raci Temizer, Director of the Museum of Anatolian Cultures at Ankara, where the Alaca and Eskiyapan material is splendidly arranged.

At Eskiyapan and a handful of other sites, objects of the same Alaca Höyük culture have come to light, and as these sites lie adjacent to the Pontic Mountains along the southern shore of the Black Sea, one of the main ore belts of Turkey, many scholars view the Alaca culture as intrusive from these regions. The Alaca tombs present many difficulties to interpretation: were these intruders Indo-Europeans, ancestors of the Hittites? Admittedly the round skulls of many of the occupants of the tombs contrast with the long heads of the ordinary population, but how significant is this in a population already mixed since Neolithic times? The type of grave, the battle-axes and the hammer-headed pins have parallels in the Pontic steppe-lands, but simple trading contact with the north through settlements on the Black Sea may have been responsible for these similarities—although the battle-axes would seem to be earlier there than in Anatolia. Then there is the clearly religious aspect of the animal figures and sun-discs from the tombs, which introduce a variety of animals—deer, bull, leopard, bird and donkey—all of which are familiar as attributes of Hattic and later Hittite deities: the bull associated with the Weather-god of Hatti, the leopard with the Sun-goddess of Arinna, the deer with the Protective (hunting) god, the donkey with Pirwa, the bird with the goddess of Kanesh (among others)—associations that go far back into the remote Anatolian past of the Neolithic.

How were these figures used before being deposited in the tombs? Were they carried on standards in procession, as some imagine, or were they fixed to funeral carts drawn by oxen, on which the dead rulers and their families were conveyed to the grave? The wooden carts with solid wheels would then presumably have been dismantled, the emblems distributed round the grave, the pairs of oxen sacrificed for a funerary meal and their heads and legs deposited on top of the tomb after the burial, as they were found, and covered with a mound of earth. Suffice to say, we simply do not know.

On the technological side, it is evident that many of the animal figures and standards were cast by the lost 'wax process', a sophisticated procedure that is also attested in Mesopotamia at this time. Many, but not all, of the objects are true tin-bronzes, which raises the old question of where did these people get their tin from. Then there are two daggers of terrestial iron, suggesting further sophisticated metallurgical techniques, unknown at this period outside Anatolia; one of them has a handle which was west Anatolian, the other has a crescentic handle that has parallels in the Royal Tombs at Ur, in Mesopotamia. Indeed, the grave-goods from Alaca Höyük show a remarkable variety and versatility of contact with neighbouring cultures, both far and near.

So do the grave goods recovered from two slightly later (EB3) tombs at Horoztepe, near Erbaa, excavated by Professor Tahsin Özgüç in the 1950s. Here we find the same combination of simple jewellery and sophisticated figurines. In addition to sun-discs and animal figures, there was an oval stool on four human legs, a metal fruitstand and a few female statuettes; one of them holds a baby and another is seated on a stool. Among the weapons are more developed swords and daggers and sophisticated shaft-held battle-axes with serrated edges, the answer to the sword and pike. Some of the metal types of this period show connections with the Mesopotamian armoury; weapons that spread from Syria before the Akkadian conquests, such as spear and pike heads with poker tangs for attachment into the wooden shafts.

The change from Early to Middle Bronze Age, corresponding in time to the fall of the Neo-Sumerian kingdom, the Third Dynasty of Ur, *c.* 2150 BC, was in western and central Anatolia a smooth transition without invasions, destructions or other signs of great catastrophe. Only in Cilicia and the east are there some signs of disturbance, probably to be connected with the appearance of Hurrian elements from across the Euphrates. The EB3 period had seen a slow development towards greater cultural unity than before and a steady amalgamation of old and new ethnic elements. In the following Middle Bronze Age these cultures were to reach a climax as Anatolia entered into trade relations with Mesopotamia, which brought great wealth, peace and understanding. Foreigners were

Bronze figure of a goddess holding a baby from Horoztepe.

Gold jug from Alaca Höyük.

welcomed and treaties between kings and merchants assured their safety. The Assyrian merchants introduced cuneiform writing, and with writing recorded history now began in Anatolia. Only in this respect can the Middle Bronze Age be regarded as a new period.

# 4

# Kültepe (Kanesh): the Middle Bronze Age 1

Some twenty-five years ago, it was commonly accepted by archaeologists that Anatolia was overrun around 1900–1800 BC by Indo-European hordes of Hittites and Luwians (ancestors of the Arzawans, Lycians, Lydians and other peoples of western Turkey), who destroyed the Early Bronze Age cultures and gradually established a new order; and that this happened at about the same time as the Greeks immigrated into Greece, destroying the Early Helladic culture there and replacing it with their own Middle Helladic one. The similarities were beguiling, and so little was known of Anatolian archaeology that there seemed no objection to fitting it into this scheme. New evidence, however, has now shown this picture to be grossly inaccurate.

The historical background to the beginning of the Middle Bronze Age in Anatolia is still to be found only in Mesopotamia. There, the energetic Kingdom of Sumer and Akkad (the Third Dynasty of Ur) had collapsed *c.* 2150 BC in a pincer movement of attacks by the Elamites from the east and invasion from the west by semi-nomadic Amorites (the Biblical name for the Amurru). This led to the establishment of Amorite dynasties at important centres like Isin, Larsa, and, particularly, Babylon. Further north, the political control that the Sumerians had exercised over Assyria was now lost, and the Old Assyrian kingdom came into being under a local dynasty (*c.* 2155–*c.* 1890 BC); this was a factor of considerable importance, as the new state was cut off from the southern copper, silver and tin supplies by the potentially unfriendly Amorite city-states, and thus tended to explore alternative sources to the north-west, in Syria and farther afield.

In Anatolia at the time of the fall of Ur, a number of significant changes are evident in the archaeological record of south-eastern Turkey. New pottery appeared, often regarded as Syrian but which may be Anatolian after all as it includes numerous beak-spouted jugs, a traditionally non-Syrian feature. There was also a number of burnings of cities like Tarsus, where different architectural plans appeared. In short, the evidence from south-east Turkey suggests that there was not simply a change of fashion, and it has been plausibly argued that the changes were occasioned by elements of the Hurrians establishing themselves there *c.* 2150 BC. The Hurrians, who were later to establish the Kingdom of Mitanni under a new Indo-Iranian dynasty in the sixteenth century BC, are found in south-eastern Anatolia from an early date, and as a working hypothesis the theory of Hurrian influence at the start of the Anatolian Middle Bronze Age will do for the present.

What happened in eastern Anatolia at this time is still a mystery, as no recognisable Middle Bronze Age pottery has yet been found east of the Keban area after the Early Bronze Age sites were deserted. Much farther to the east, however, beyond the Turkish frontier in the Trialeti uplands above Tiflis, a distinct class of EB3 pottery is found in great stone tumuli with cart burials, which many archaeologists interpret as in intrusion of Indo-European elements from the north Caucasian steppe. This is followed by a Middle Bronze Age phase of fine pottery. The evidence in Trialeti, mainly from graves, suggests a peaceful change, and one that led to great prosperity, as witnessed by the amount of jewellery and gold and silver vessels and daggers. It is tempting to see this region as the base from which came the Indo-Iranian overlords of the Hurrians.

Changes in central Anatolia are better documented; the gaily-painted Cappadocian ware of EB3 lived on, now accompanied by a superior wheel-made monochrome ware, brilliantly burnished in plum red and other colours. With it occur plain wheel-made cups and beakers of Syrian inspiration, which had been common in Cilicia during all the Early Bronze Age but are new arrivals on the Anatolian plateau. The origin of the new wheel-made burnished ware needs much more investigation; there is still a great deal of argument about the interpretation of apparent parallels found in other sites. The evidence of pottery has often been misused in order to demonstrate migrations or conquests, but pottery styles can travel along trade-routes without ethnic implications, or they can be produced by itinerant potters and tinkers. My personal opinion is that we are not

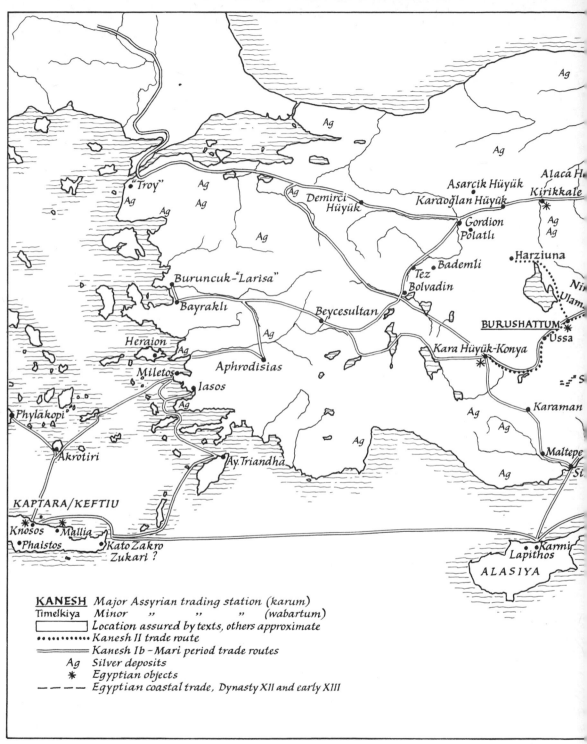

KANESH — Major Assyrian trading station (karum)
Timelkiya — Minor " " " (wabartum)
▭ — Location assured by texts, others approximate
•••••••• — Kanesh II trade route
═══ — Kanesh Ib – Mari period trade routes
Ag — Silver deposits
✳ — Egyptian objects
– – – – — Egyptian coastal trade, Dynasty XII and early XIII

The Middle Bronze
Age I—climax of
international trade.

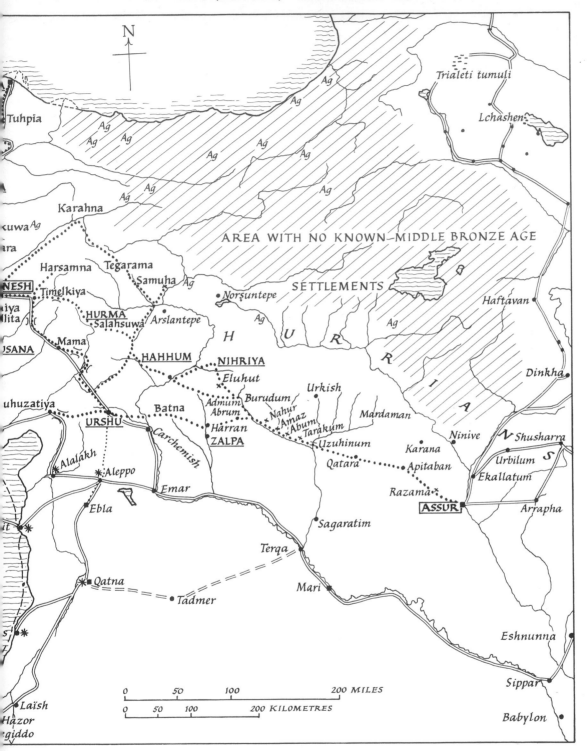

N

Tuhpia

Trialeti tumuli

Lchashen

Ag
Ag
Ag
Ag
Ag
Ag
Ag
Ag

Karahna

kuwa Ag

ara

AREA WITH NO KNOWN MIDDLE BRONZE AGE

Harsamna    Tegarama

SETTLEMENTS

Samuha Ag

NESH

iya
lita

Timelkiya

Norşuntepe

Haftavan

Ag

HURMA
Salahsuwa    Arslantepe

Ag

Ag

USANA    Mama

H        U        R

Dinkha

HAHHUM    NIHRIYA

R

Eluhut

Urkish

I

Burudum

Admum  Abrum  Nahur  Amaz  Tarakum
uhuzatiya    Batna    Abum

Mardaman    A

Ninive    Shusharra

URSHU    Härran    Uzuhinum

S

Carchemish    ZALPA

Karana

Urbilum

Qatara    Apitaban

Ekallatum

Alalakh    Razama    x

Aleppo    Emar

ASSUR    Arrapha

Ebla

it

Sagaratim

Terqa

Qatna

Mari

Tädmer

Eshnunna

S

Laïsh    Sippar

Hazor

giddo    Babylon

0        50        100        200 MILES
0    50    100        200 KILOMETRES

dealing here with a diffusion *from* central Anatolia and that the wheel-made Syrian plain wares clearly came from the east along a southern trade route.

To sum up: the beginning of the Middle Bronze Age in Anatolia saw a number of changes and although there is little doubt that cultural continuity was dominant in many places, there is equally good evidence for a 'wind of change', at least, and less isolation. The old theory of a complete break between Early and Middle Bronze Age must therefore be abandoned, and with it the idea that it was Hittite and Luwian invaders who established a new culture pattern in Anatolia.

What really distinguished the Middle Bronze Age in Anatolia was the development of widespread trade contacts with Mesopotamia, spearheaded by the arrival of large numbers of Assyrian merchants who were allowed to set up a trading network throughout central Anatolia sometime between 2050–2000 BC. This opened up Anatolia to Assyrian trade and drew the country into the orbit of the old civilisations of Mesopotamia. Although Indo-Europeans with writing of their own were already established in south-western Anatolia at this time, as shown by the so-called 'Hittite' hieroglyphic seal from Beycesultan (*c*. 2000 BC), the Assyrian newcomers introduced writing in Assyrian cuneiform on clay tablets. These are the oldest surviving literary records from Anatolia and they give us, for the first time, a vivid insight into the society of the period. From 2000 BC, Anatolian rulers (and their subjects) could communicate with each other in writing, theoretically at least.

The key site for this fascinating period of Anatolian archaeology, that of the Assyrian trading settlements, is Kültepe (ancient Kanesh), near Kayseri in Cappadocia, in central Turkey. It has been excavated since 1948 by Tahsin and Nimet Özgüç of Ankara University, their assistant Kutlu Emre and the Assyriologist Kemal Balkan. Through systematic research and great perseverance, they have revealed a vital period of Anatolia's greatness. (The two ladies of the team have followed up the work at Kültepe by equally spectacular results at the great mound of Acemköy, which may well be the ancient city of Burushattum/Puruskhanda, associated in Mesopotamian legend with Sargon of Akkad.) Frequent mention of a trading post at Kanesh has now been discovered in the texts of the city of Ebla, seventy kilometres south of Aleppo, destroyed by Sargon's grandson, Narasin, in the twenty-fourth century BC.

The two archaeological levels relevant to this period are

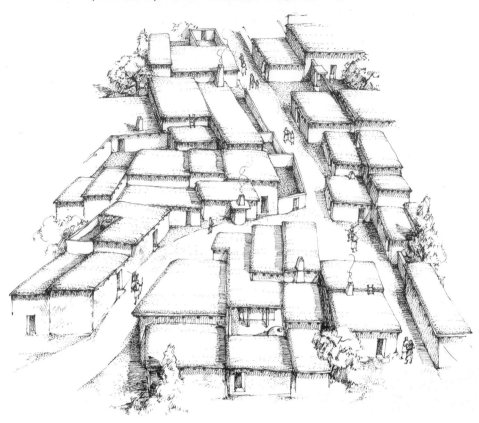

Reconstruction of houses in the trading quarter of Kanesh II.

Kültepe/Kanesh II and its following phase, Ib. Kanesh II was destroyed *c.* 1940 BC, and was rebuilt after an interval in undiminished splendour—the Ib phase—although with apparently fewer resident Assyrian merchants.

Excavations have revealed that the trading area (*karum*) or bazaar of Kanesh occupied an area some 500 metres wide around a walled citadel that had been established on an Early Bronze Age mound and was itself surrounded by strong fortifications. The citadel contained the king's palaces and perhaps some temples and the houses of his ministers; the *karum* was the headquarters of Assyrian and native merchants, some of them men of Kanesh, others traders from different Anatolian states, grouped in quarters or living side by side. There was no segregation, and interspersed with the houses, rich and poor alike, were eating-houses or taverns; according to the cuneiform texts there were also temples and shrines of Assyrian and local gods, although none has yet been discovered. Streets and alleys separated blocks of houses of different sizes, and there was no standard plan. The Assyrians clearly enjoyed local culture and, but for their

Impression from a
Middle Bronze Age
Kanesh seal with
double eagle.

inscribed seals and clay tablets, they were archaeologically in-distinguishable from the Anatolians. They lived very comfortably under the protection of the Anatolian kings, often had local wives, slaves and slave-girls and were fully integrated into the society of the day. They had their own officials, through whom they exercised their own jurisdiction over their fellow-Assyrians and ran the whole network of Assyrian trade in central Anatolia; but they were subject to Anatolian laws and goodwill and paid taxes to the Anatolian kings.

The fire and destruction that overtook Kanesh around 1940 BC has proved a great blessing to archaeologists. In the rush to save their lives, the Assyrian merchants left everything behind except their valuables; yet for the archaeologist, the clay tablets they abandoned were the most precious of all. Without them, we would not even have known that Assyrians had lived in Kanesh. Nor would we have inherited such a wealth of evidence about Anatolian society, geography, economics and trade.

Historical information in the Kanesh texts (nearly all of which are business transactions), is, alas, limited. Assyrian trade started late in the reign of King Erisum of Assur and three generations of Assyrian merchants left their tablets, covering 86 years. But they tell us a little about the central Anatolian hierarchy: a Great King resides in Burushattum, and all other rulers are mere kings, including the king of Kanesh. After the ruler, the chief official is the crown prince, who bears the title 'Chief of the Citadel' (i.e. the keeper of the treasury or the palace store-rooms) and he also has judiciary powers. Below king and crown prince come a host of dignitaries: palace officials like mace-bearer, major-domo and butler, the superior of the lay priests and the military: commanders of the guards, the divisional commander, the chief of the chariots and the keeper of the arsenal. In charge of the agricultural economy are chiefs of cattle, goats, horses, herds; a chief gardener and one of vegetables. Industry is headed by chiefs of metal-founders, bronze workers, of some undefined metal objects, and a distributor of metals. In charge of trade were chiefs of tradesmen, cloth, warehouses, the market, millers (?), an adviser or banker (?) to the distributor of metals, and (important in this cosmopolitan society) a chief of interpreters, the word for which still survives in Turkish.

The whole purpose of sending Assyrian merchants to Anatolia was to ensure a steady supply of Anatolian silver and some gold (iron and precious stones were not allowed out of Anatolia) in exchange for tin and garments. These commodities were transported by caravans of black donkeys bred in Assyria. The Assyrians made 75–100% profit on the tin, and 100% profit on the cloth. Freight was cheap but taxes were heavy, and though most of them were paid to Assyrian officials and ploughed back into the enterprise, taxes and transport accounted for nearly half the cargo. When a caravan arrived at Kanesh from Assyria, it would enter the palace of the ruler and some of the merchandise would be retained as customs and toll duties; then the palace and high dignitaries would buy a certain quantity, paying in silver or using Assyrian credit, and the remainder would be released for sale in the *karum* by the Assyrian merchants or carried further by them to other Anatolian states. The Assyrians also traded in copper in central Anatolia, but did not export it to Assur. In case of debt the palace would confiscate the goods. The quantities traded could be considerable: a cargo of 410 talents (over 12 tons) of tin is once mentioned, and we hear of 150 tons of copper, or consignments of 100 or even 200 garments, but these are the exceptions. Markets for copper, silver and iron are mentioned, but the latter was used only in very small quantities at this time, probably just for ornaments. Silver was 130 times the price of copper, gold 7–9 times the price of silver, and an offer for iron at 8 times the price of gold was not considered acceptable. Tin prices are not mentioned—which is strange, as tin was the most essential import. In the following table, 60 shekels of silver = 1 mina, c. half a kilo:

Seal impression of Minoan affinity from Kara Hüyük, Konya.

| A sack of barley | 1 shekel |
| A sack of wheat | 2–2⅓ shekels |
| A lamb | ⅓–1 shekel |
| A sheep | 1–5 shekels |
| A slave child | 5–10 shekels |
| A cow or donkey | 20–30 shekels |
| A slave girl | 20–30 shekels |
| A male slave | 30–45 shekels |

Seal impression of Persian gulf type.

Trade with Assyria was only a section of a much longer chain that extended westwards to Crete and the Aegean and eastwards to Iran, Central Asia and the Indus Valley—long-range trade indeed, dependent on a great number of treaties and much goodwill or commercial common sense all round.

Judging by the texts, Kanesh was a city of spectacular wealth, of which archaeology only brings us faint echoes. Metalwork consisted of gold, silver and bronze vessels, socketed spear-heads, axes, pins with melon heads, toggle-pins, seals, a bronze trolley on wheels, copper ingots and gold skull-caps. Vessels made of rock crystal or obsidian, textile fragments embroidered with gold wire, figurines of faience and ivory—they only give the merest glimpse of life at the time. Cylinder-seals and stamp-seals mark an apogee in glyptic art and testify to foreign trade-links with Mesopotamia, Syria, even Crete. And this wealth and artistic creativity were by no means confined to Kanesh.

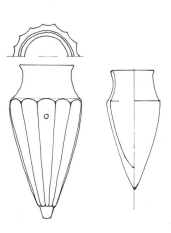

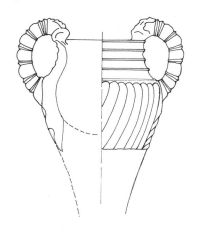

Rock crystal (left) and obsidian (right) vessels from the palace at Acemköy.

The archaeological remains of the two phases of what is frequently called the 'Assyrian colony period' (Kanesh II and Ib in archaeological terms) mark the climax of central Anatolian culture, heir and descendant of the local Early Bronze Age. After the destruction of Kanesh II around 1940 BC, Kanesh Ib flourished again, after an interval, until *c.* 1875 BC. Trade was re-established with Assyria, where the Amorite King Shamshi-Adad I (1953–1921 BC) ruled from the foothills of the Taurus to the Zagros Mountains. His name is found at Kanesh and Acemköy and after his death Zimrilim of Mari continued trading with Anatolia. Then came the destruction of Mari by Hammurabi of Babylon *c.* 1897 BC and trade ceased. Accustomed to wealth, local kings, faced with ever decreasing profits, turned to the only alternative course open to them in order to fill their coffers—plunder and conquest. Anitta, King of Kussara, set out to conquer central Anatolia with an army of 1,400 men and 40 chariots—and from Kanesh he subdued most of his rivals including Burushattum, the seat of the Great King, and Hattus, the later Hittite capital, which he cursed.

Thus began a period of wars and conquests, destruction and devastation which in the course of a few generations reduced central Anatolia, once rich, to a land of ruins. From these ruins emerge a people who were to make their mark not only upon the region but on the Western cultural consciousness—the Hittites.

The Assyrian clay tablets of the Kanesh II and Ib periods contained thousands of personal names ranging from kings to slaves, which give unmistakable clues to the ethnic composition of the local population. From an analysis of only a fraction of the evidence, it appears that speakers of Indo-European were already fully established throughout central Anatolia and several kings bear Indo-European names. Other evidence suggests that the arrival and spread of Indo-European speakers can be dated from *c.* 2700 BC onwards. Those who settled in central Anatolia seem well integrated with the old Hattic society in the region of Hatti, with its capital at Hattus. From this old society, the newcomers earned the name of 'Hittites'. There are indications that they were not at all what we might expect Indo-Europeans to be. First, they called themselves after the land in which they settled—Men of Hatti, or Pala, or Luwia—instead of imposing their own tribal names which they somehow managed to lose. Not less surprising is their reaction to Hattic religion; they chose the old Sun-goddess of Arinna (Wurusemu = Earth-mother) as the supreme deity of the Hittite state, something not done among orthodox Indo-Europeans, who normally had a male god like Zeus or Jupiter at the head of their pantheon. He did exist, but in a subordinate role as Weather-god of Hatti, husband of the Sun-goddess, and may have been called 'God' Siuna (cf. Zeus) or Tarhun(d)a, a modified form of his Hattic name Taru, whose symbol was a bull (*tauros*). Both deities are clearly fertility gods in spite of the goddess's title. None of this fits into what Indo-European theory would expect us to find—a splendid example of the uselessness of preconceived or predicted 'models' or theories. The Hittites and Luwians even managed to lose many common Indo-European words like 'father' and 'mother', and adopted local words for mother ('anna' and 'anni') and father ('atta' and 'tatti'). To use a common expression, it seems that the Indo-Europeans in Anatolia had 'gone native', but only up to a point; they kept their languages, on the whole, and it was the earlier tongues that gradually disappeared.

Their arrival or at least that of the Hittites seems to have been relatively peaceful. The idea of a wholesale Indo-European takeover or conquest is rapidly fading and although the way in which they entered Turkey remains uncertain (one suspects the usual pattern of alliance, intermarriage, infiltration, occasional brute force and conquest, assassination and mercenary revolts—a series of crimes we

Impression of the
Tyszkiewicz seal, a
Middle Bronze Age
cylinder-seal.

euphemistically call history), the Hittite rise to power was gradual and belongs to the period *after* the breakdown of the Assyrian trade.

The Kanesh II texts provide us with our first geographical picture of central Anatolia and the routes to the Euphrates—generally speaking the same area as the later Old Hittite kingdom, the political heir of fifteen or more city-states of the trading period. Only five of these were powerful enough to be called 'lands': Burushattum, Kanesh, Hattum, Zalpa and Wahsusana, all west of the Antitaurus. In the mountains, there were smaller principalities ruled by kings or occasionally queens, small fry compared to their western neighbours.

The wholesale destruction at the end of the Assyrian colony period gave the Hittites their opportunity to attain power. Anitta, although probably not a Hittite himself, became the prototype of the conqueror and set a pattern of endemic warfare in Anatolia that did not cease until Cyrus the Persian established the *pax persica* in 546 BC.

Most of the great central Anatolian mounds belong to the trading rather than to the following, Hittite, period and there can now be no doubts that what is known as Hittite civilisation had its roots here. The elaborate religious scenes on cylinder-seals of the period are ancestors of the Hittite reliefs (and wall-paintings if they existed). The splendid vessels of animal shape inspired Hittite metal vessels as well as clay and stone sculpture. Hittite pottery is merely an impoverished reflection of the incredibly rich and varied ceramic repertoire of the Colony period.

The idea of writing in cuneiform on clay tablets came to the Hittites from the Assyrians, but when they eventually came to write, they borrowed a later Babylonian form of the script current in north Syria. Horses and chariots, which were to become the mainstay of the later Hittite armies, are already seen on pots in Kanesh II and recorded in the texts. Whatever level of culture the Indo-Europeans might have had before they entered Turkey, they fell completely

OPPOSITE
Red burnished jug
imitating metal vessel
from Kültepe.

54

under the spell of what they found in Anatolia and, to mix metaphors, became 'more Christian than the Pope', shedding all traces of a now despised background as soon as they could, except for their language and certain social customs. Potentially bright pupils, the Hittites were fortunate to receive the best possible cultural education from their Hattic teachers at the climax of their ancient greatness.

Kültepe II tablet in inscribed clay 'envelope'.

# 5

# The Hittite Old Kingdom: Middle Bronze Age 2

At the end of the Assyrian trading period, *c.* 1875 BC, many of the once-prosperous Hattic cities lay in ruins, burnt and deserted, or else sheltering a mere fraction of their former populations squatting in half-repaired buildings. Some, like Hattus, had been destroyed and cursed by Anitta, who had tried to consolidate his rule over central Anatolia; but the destruction of Anitta's new capital of Kanesh/Nesa (Kültepe Ib), and the total darkness that surrounds his fate and that of his successors, suggest that his efforts had come to nothing.

Around *c.* 1785, a century after the death of Anitta, a powerful ruler called Hattusili I, king of Kussara (Anitta's original kingdom), ignored the curse that Anitta had placed on Hattus and rebuilt it as his capital, now called Hattusa (modern Boğazköy). Many scholars regard him as the first Hittite king and we have contemporary records of his reign, written in old Hittite and Akkadian. Later texts refer to a certain Labarna as the founder of the Hittite Old Kingdom; but as this is a title borne by all Hittite kings (including Hattusili), the pseudo-historical Labarna and the historical king Hattusili are regarded by some scholars as one and the same person, but I doubt this.

Of Labarna it is said that in his days the Hittite land was small, but that he extended the frontiers to the Black Sea and the Mediterranean. More specifically, Labarna took the great cities of the 'Lower Land' between the Halys River and the Taurus Mountains, and installed his sons as governors. He also fought against 'the lands of Arzawa and Wilusa' (western Anatolia) and is said to have subdued them. These legendary conquests, whether accomplished by Hattusili I or Labarna, or for that matter collectively by earlier Hittite kings before Hattusili's reign, would suggest a territory not much larger

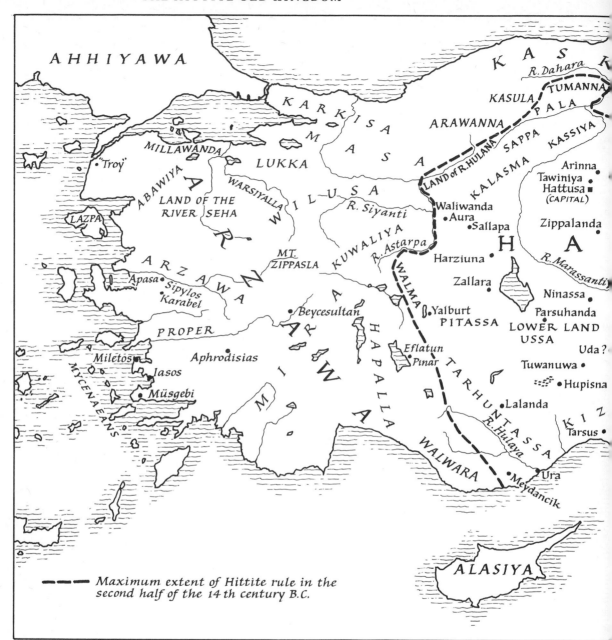

Anatolian political geography in the second millennium BC.

than that of Anitta's as a base for further expansion. Precisely how the Hittite dynasty rose to power in Anitta's ancestral kingdom of Kussara, no text explains; usurpation, assassination or succession through marriage suggest themselves as various possibilities. The site of Kussara itself has not been located; Alişar Hüyük has been suggested, or a location in the Divriği area near the Euphrates.

Our first historical text, Hattusili I's bilingual Annals, record five

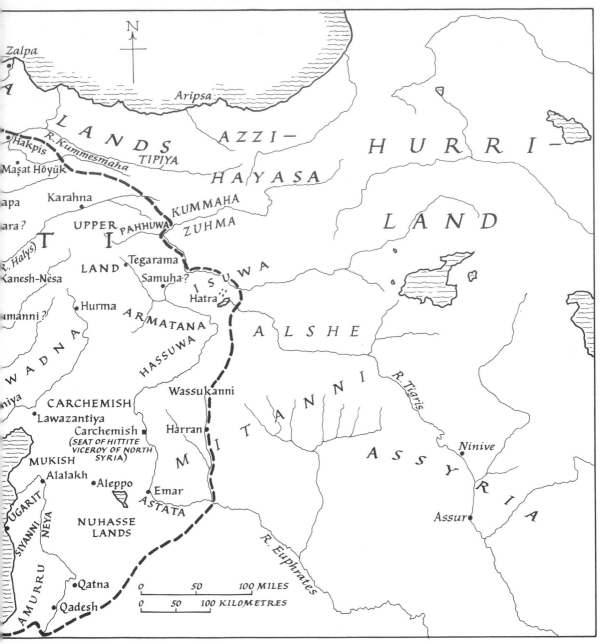

years of warfare, destruction and plunder in a candid and factual account, very possibly at the beginning of his reign but after Hattusa had become the new capital. The pattern of warfare is of some interest as it would tend to repeat itself throughout Hittite history: as long as the Hittite king was at home in the land of Hatti, the formerly independent city-states were quiescent—but when he went on a campaign outside the country, other enemies would enter Hatti and the Hittite cities revolted against the king, 'and only Hattusa, a single city, remained'. Hittite rule was based on conquest, and on the legal fiction of 'once conquered, forever Hittite'—a view, needless to say, that was not shared by the victims of Hittite aggression, and often fiercely resisted.

Such resistance led to the destruction of the city involved, which would be burnt and have its gods carried off to Hattusa or Arinna, the great cult centre, and placed in the temples of the Sun-goddess or her daughter. What happened to the population is less clear; some may have been deported to Hittite lands, others left to rebuild their city, and sometimes garrisons were installed to keep them in order. With their power broken, many old cities survived into later Hittite times only as cult centres with a depleted population (Kanesh-Nesa and Puruskhanda, for instance); many others were reduced to *tells*, dead cities then as now dotting the monotonous landscape of central Anatolia, vantage-points only for shepherds and their dogs, haunted places under the protection of the Weather-god of the *tells*. We have no evidence that the Hittites established farms in the territories of the destroyed cities, but we frequently hear of sheep-folds, and the long lists of minor settlements do suggest that walled cities that were destroyed in conflict were often replaced by rural villages.

Hittite wealth was concentrated in the capital and a few great cities in central Hatti, or in important strategic centres or cult cities like Arinna. This redistribution of wealth had profound effects on the Hittite economy; the centralisation of power deprived the provinces, and feudal estates destroyed the splendid developments in trade and industry that were seen during the Assyrian trade period. The result of this concentration of wealth and power in a few prosperous centres, such as the colossal city of Hattusa, was that the rural countryside was starved. One can hardly escape the conclusion that the Hittites effectively managed to ruin central Anatolia, and many of their neighbours as well; and it was Hattusili I, the founder of the Old Kingdom, who accelerated the economic decline that had set in with the breakdown of the international trade of the Kültepe period and Anitta's conquests a century earlier.

Hattusili's wars are of interest because they set the pattern of Hittite military and economic strategy. To the north he destroyed his rivals, the city of Sanahuitta and the land of Zalpa, because they lay on the route from the Hittite capital to the Black Sea, where he could get a foothold on the coast and possible maritime trade connections with a tin route to Central Europe. To the west he attacked Arzawa and/or

Wilusa (according to a later version), no doubt from a desire to control also the western land route by which tin could be transported to Hatti.

But it was to the east and south that his main efforts and achievements were concentrated, against those lands that barred the approach to the Euphrates and northern Syria, which was then dominated by the Hurrian kingdom of Halab (Aleppo). The first attack fell on Alalakh (Tell Atchana), in the Plain of Antioch beside the River Orontes, which was destroyed. This city, which was excavated by Sir Leonard Woolley before and after the Second World War, was a dependency of Aleppo, and controlled the Mediterranean exit of the Euphrates trade route. Woolley found archaeological evidence of Hattusili's attack in the burnt ruins of Alalakh VII.

The next to fall was the old city of Urshu, the centre of the timber trade to Mesopotamia, to be followed by the destruction of the land of Hassuwa across the Euphrates. Hattusili boasts that no one before him had crossed that river, except Sargon of Akkad coming from the opposite direction. Thus in a few short years, Hattusili appears to have extended the frontiers of Hatti to the Black Sea and the Mediterranean, and to the east bank of the Euphrates—something that none of his ancestors had achieved and that all his successors wanted to emulate. They were remarkable achievements indeed for a new and obscure Indo-European dynasty.

But Aleppo, the 'White City', the bastion of Syria, was unconquered, and so the focal point of the Mesopotamian tin route to the east, essential to any Bronze Age economy, was not yet his. According to a later text, Hattusili was wounded in an attack on Aleppo, and his blood was avenged by his successor. The text called Hattusili's Testament portrays Hattusili as an old and embittered king by then, betrayed by his family and subjects and with none of his sons left alive, appointing his grandson Mursili I as heir to the throne, telling him how to live and rule and flourish, and beseeching him, when the time comes, to hold the dead king to his breast and consign him to the earth. This passage, coming from that harsh conqueror, still strikes a chord today, and shows that in times of personal distress, Hittite rulers could behave and feel like normal human beings in need of sympathy.

Mursili I (1746–1738) has left us no contemporary Hittite records, but his military exploits would have delighted his grandfather. He conquered Aleppo, and thus became master of northern Syria. He marched against Babylonia, 700 kilometres down the Euphrates, perhaps with the help of the Kassite dynasty established midway at

Khana. He took Babylon and sacked it, *c.* 1738 BC, thus putting an end to the dynasty of Hammurabi and ushering in a period of Kassite rule of Babylonia.

Laden with booty, which included statues of Marduk and other Babylonian deities, Mursili was attacked by the Hurrians on his homeward march. He jettisoned the gods of Babylon with his allies at Khana and got back safely to Hattusa, only to be murdered there by his brother-in-law Hantili, who thereby succeeded to the throne. Nemesis followed upon hubris as night follows day; and the ephemeral might of the Old Hittite Kingdom established by Labarna (?), Hattusili and Mursili came toppling down in the days of Hantili, the regicide.

Out of the mountains of the north-west came a fierce tribal race called the Kaska. These tribes severed once and for all the short-lived Hittite access to the Black Sea coast. They occupied Nerik, one of the great Hittite cult centres, and spread throughout the Pontic Mountains all along the northern edge of the Hittite lands on either side of the Halys River. They were not content simply to establish themselves there, thus depriving the Hittites of the rich metal mines of the Pontic Mountains; on the contrary, their aim was the conquest of the Hittite homeland itself. Thus, from the days of Hantili, the Hittites acquired yet another enemy to contend with, resolute and vigilant but tribal and disunited; the Kaska waged a kind of guerrilla warfare, burning Hittite harvests, destroying and harrying, making all northern Hatti unsafe. They were elusive and never admitted defeat, however sorely they were mauled by punitive Hittite expeditions, until they achieved their aim around 1200 BC with the conquest of the Hittite homeland. Who the Kaska were nobody knows, but I suspect that they were further tribes of Indo-European people, like the Hittites themselves, coming from the west and infiltrating along the easterly trend of the Pontic Mountains. Ironically, it was the Hittite destruction by Hattusili of the kingdom of Zalpa that may have broken the last barrier that restrained them.

Hantili's reign was long remembered as a disastrous one, and Hittite territory soon shrank like a deflated balloon. Military disasters provoked internal strife, and a long succession of palace murders weakened whatever was left of the Hittite state. It was not until a century after Mursili's death that Telepinu, one of the last kings of the Old Kingdom, succeeded in restoring order both at home and abroad.

Much of the previous history of the Hittite state comes from a pseudo-historical edict of this king, the so-called Telepinu Text.

Nothing suggests that Telepinu was a great warrior; in a list of 'revolting' territories we find all the old familiar enemies — Arzawa to the west, Adaniya in Cilicia on the south coast, Hassuwa across the Euphrates. Not only was he back to where Hattusili had started, he now had the Kaska to reckon with as well, almost visible on the northern horizon from his citadel at Hattusa.

The four or five kings who followed Telepinu have sometimes been combined into a 'Middle Kingdom', an unnecessary subdivision of no historical or archaeological substance. All the kings are obscure, and the three last ones who may not have existed are only 'known' from offering-lists of later descendants. Historically, the only evidence from their reigns consists of fragments of treaties made with the kings of Kizzuwadna (Cilicia) if correctly assigned; these treaties were intended to ensure Hittite control of the passes leading to northern Syria, which was now lost and constituted a potential danger of Hurrian encroachment. Hittite political power was in full decline.

From an archaeological point of view, the period of the Hittite Old Kingdom is distinguished by a general poverty of remains that comes as a shock after the wealth of material from the Assyrian trading period. Economic decline and incessant warfare had taken a heavy toll. Also, the Old Kingdom buildings were replaced by the more ambitious structures of later kings, and little of them remains except for a few disconnected palace walls within powerful city walls with gates and posterns.

At Alaca Höyük (Arinna?), near Boğazköy, the site of the spectacular 'Royal Tombs' of the Early Bronze Age (cf. Ch 3), a magnificent monumental gateway of the Old Kingdom period still stands, flanked by two great sphinxes and decorated with crude stone reliefs (probably once stuccoed and painted), illustrating lively scenes of hunting and religious activities accompanied by merrymaking — probably the earliest Hittite sculptures that have survived. These scenes are closely related to polychrome-painted relief-decorated pottery cult vessels like the famous Bitik and Inandik vases. The latter was found in a temple excavated by R. Temizer (but still unpublished), which can be dated by a tablet of the time of Hattusili I; so this style of sculpture was characteristic of the Hittite rise to power. Its origins are clear: they lie in the finely engraved scenes of stone cylinder seals from Kanesh (Kültepe II), and the stamp seals of Kanesh-Nesa (Kültepe Ib), some of which were made in precious metal. The double eagle carved on the Alaca Höyük gate, adopted as the symbol of Hittite kingship, goes back to the same period.

OPPOSITE
Libation vase from
Kültepe II in the form
of a lion.

Silver rhyton or
libation vase, with
religious scene, in the
form of a stag,
attributed to the Old
Hittite period.

Other cult vessels are ornamented with bulls' heads and may, as so often in Anatolia, reflect metal prototypes. Two splendid silver rhytons, one in the form of a resting bull, the other a stag, are chance finds from central Anatolia, and the bull can be matched in a clay version from near Kirşehir that has been assigned to the period of the Old Kingdom. The edge of the stag rhyton bears an elaborate religious scene with various deities arranged like those on the clay vessels. Moreover, some of the deities are identified by hieroglyphic inscriptions in gold, and may be roughly dated to the period of Telepinu, the last king of the Old Kingdom. Such splendid workmanship in silver and gold, and the polychrome-painted pottery and stone carving, show that the Hittites were clearly able to innovate on the old Hattic culture with striking artistic success. The same originality is seen in some of their seals, probably made in gold, whose impressions have survived.

Old Hittite pottery, on the other hand, suffered a marked decline compared to earlier excellence, except in cult vessels; and this in itself is explicable if the court and the rich mainly used metalware, while pottery copies were assigned to the kitchen or left to the poor. This

Polychrome relief vase from Bitik showing religious scenes, Hittite Old Kingdom.

differentiation between what was used by various classes becomes much more distinct as time goes on, and offers a marked contrast to the happier age at the beginning of the second millennium when everyone, both high and low, enjoyed the best craftsmanship. Not surprisingly, perhaps, the potters were still working in the old Kültepe tradition, but the exuberant decoration of earlier times has gone, the number of shapes is restricted, and most of the pots are purely utilitarian and dull beyond belief.

Another factor which has severely curtailed the recovery of archaeological remains was the introduction of cremation, which ruled out rich burial gifts. This was by no means universal, but no rich tombs have yet been found. It is often stated that the Hittite kings practised cremation, but this may have been only a later custom, since Hattusili I entreated his grandson Mursili to 'consign him to the earth'—not the flames. Cremation graves excavated at the Hittite capital are frequently accompanied by the skulls of horses and, at most, a few pots. Of the armament of the period, archaeology has failed to inform us so far. For a span of some 350 years, this is a rather poor record, and it should stimulate further research on early Hittite sites like Inandik that are not burdened or disturbed by later deposits.

Silver rhyton in the form of a bull attributed to the Old Hittite period.

# 6

# The Hittite
# New Kingdom

When Tudhaliya I, the founder of the Hittite New Kingdom, came to
the throne *c.* 1475 BC, after a long period of obscurity and decline
from which no historical records have survived, the 'Hurrian
interval', significant changes had taken place on the Near Eastern
scene. The Hurrians had become a power to be reckoned with, and
had established the kingdom of Mitanni, whose territories stretched
throughout northern Mesopotamia and eastern Anatolia to the
Zagros Mountains in the east and the Caucasus in the north. The king
of Mitanni at this time was Saussatar. His capital lay at Wassukanni,
still unidentified but not far east of the Euphrates, and strategically
placed to exercise control over Syria. On the far western horizon he
could have seen the blue mountains of the Taurus, once firmly in
Hittite hands; but for over a century now no Hittite king had even
approached the Euphrates, and a powerful buffer state, Kizzuwadna
(Cilicia), protected his north-western flank, under its king Sunassura I.
Another vassal held the land of Isuwa, east of the Euphrates on the
high plateau guarding the eastern routes from Hatti and the great
copper mines of Ergani above Diyarbakir. The state of Mitanni was
rich and prosperous; it held all the trade routes to the east, and it was
ruled by a vigorous dynasty of Indo-Iranian speakers, though most of
its subjects were Hurrians. Assyria was a Mitannian vassal, while
Babylonia was independent under its Kassite rulers and politically
inactive. Hurrian influence was also strong in Hatti itself.

But there was another formidable new power in the area—Egypt.
Under the aggressive and energetic Pharaoh Tuthmosis III
(1504–1450), Egypt had become a major imperial power, and Syria,
the Hittites' Promised Land, was rapidly being turned into an

Egyptian province. Tuthmosis III records that in the west his power reached as far as Keftiu (Crete) and Assuwa, which seems to have lain north of the land of Arzawa, the enemy on the western flank of Hatti. Envoys from both Crete and Assuwa are recorded as bringing precious gifts to Egypt at this time, which shows that both nations were engaged in trade with Syria and therefore anxious to establish good relations with its new master, Tuthmosis III, whose fleet controlled the coast.

The auspices for the birth of the Hittite New Kingdom were hardly favourable. The arch-enemy, Arzawa, menaced Hatti from the west, and archaeological evidence suggests that its power, prosperity and perhaps also its population were growing rapidly from *c.* 1500 BC. Mitanni held the east; Syria to the south was in Egyptian hands, and to the north, the Kaska were a constant threat. All the valuable trade routes that Hittite kings had always striven to control had slipped from their grasp.

Yet somehow, remarkably, Tudhaliya I managed it. During his reign the new ruler, whose ancestry is unknown, was able to re-establish Hittite power and pull it sharply out of its decline. He made war against Arzawa, he destroyed Assuwa, and he repelled the Kaska. Then, with his rear secured, he attacked the Hurrians in Isuwa across the Euphrates. He made a treaty with Kizzuwadna to open the way to Syria, and then in 1465 concluded an agreement with Tuthmosis III over Syria and entered Aleppo, like Mursili I nearly three hundred years earlier. The old dream had come true, the Hittite king once again held the two great trade routes.

The Hittite New Kingdom is frequently referred to as the 'Hittite Empire', a term which was coined before its history was properly understood and one which greatly exaggerates its power. It obscures the inherent weaknesses of the Hittite political system, which was based as before not on an efficient military and civil service administering conquered territories (a prerequisite for empire), but on the martial prestige and abilities of the ruler and his capacity to maintain his suzerainty over unwilling subjects temporarily reduced to the status of protected territories or vassals. The Hittite state was neither an empire nor a confederation; it was a totalitarian state with treaties imposed by force on defeated peoples.

The Hittite records, fortunately, are often specific or naive enough to allow one to read between the lines and separate the facts from the political dogma. The picture that emerges is much less grandiose than that presented in the past; instead of a Hittite suzerain ruling Turkey

Rock sanctuary of
Yazılıkaya just outside
the Hittite capital of
Hattusa.

from Lake Van to the Aegean from his capital at Hattusa, one finds a
whole group of states, some large, some small, constantly disputing
possession of the Anatolian plateau with the Hittites, who are
surrounded by enemies and have no friends. The Hittites found Syria
relatively easy to hold; its states were small and divided, and
unwarlike. But the mountainous Anatolian plateau was inhabited by
peoples very much like themselves, tenacious and hardy and
unwilling to accept Hittite chains and slavery. Hittite success on the
plateau depended very much on the prowess of neighbouring rulers;
when strong, their position in the centre enabled the Hittites to strike
at enemies one at a time. Their control of the centre effectively
prevented concerted action by several enemies, provided that Hittite
defences were strong; when they were not, Hatti was easily invaded
from all sides, and even the capital and main cities of Hatti were
vulnerable to attack. Such attacks from all sides invariably greeted the
accession of a new king, and their repulse kept Hittite kings busy for

years or even decades on end. The drain on Hittite manpower must have been severe, and later Hittite kings took to deporting massive populations from conquered states as agricultural slaves to Hatti. Eventually the Hittites, like the Spartans, would disappear through lack of manpower.

The see-sawing of Hittite power went on throughout the New Kingdom period. Not long after the founder, Tudhaliya I, had re-established Hittite prestige, Hatti was on its knees again, overrun by Arzawan forces from the west and Kaska tribesmen from the north, its capital sacked and burned.

Hatti would have perished there and then but for the efforts of Prince Suppiluliuma, probably the greatest of Hittite warriors. In years of fighting he once again re-established Hittite power, and when he ascended the throne *c.* 1380 the land of Hatti had been cleared of invaders. Beyond the old frontiers, though, he was less successful, and Arzawa remained independent. He then turned to Syria and spent the rest of his life in its conquest, giving the reconstituted state new life through loot and plunder, though neglecting Anatolian affairs. An Egyptian campaign by his eldest son, the crown prince, who penetrated into the Lebanon *c.* 1350, had disastrous results in that it brought to Anatolia the plague that was to ravage war-torn Hatti for twenty years, claiming the old king Suppiluliuma and his successor as its first victims.

When his younger son, Mursili II, ascended the throne in 1345 BC the situation in Anatolia was as grave as that which had confronted his father, although Syria was securely held from the big Hittite base at Carchemish, where Mursili's brother held sway. It took Mursili a dozen years to re-establish Hittite power; the manpower shortage was alleviated by the incorporation of Kizzuwadna (Cilicia) into the Hittite state, and the army at Carchemish was called in to help in a great campaign against Arzawa. Mursili eventually succeeded in taking the Arzawan capital (the only Hittite king known to have done so) and allegedly deporting 100,000 civilian prisoners. In his later years his main anxiety must have been the resurgence of Egyptian power under the vigorous Pharaohs of the Nineteenth Dynasty, who had their eyes on Syria. A trial of strength between Egypt and the Hittites over Syria was obviously on the way.

Mursili died before this happened, and his son Muwatalli was on the throne when Rameses II led a large Egyptian army northward just after 1300 BC. Muwatalli headed a Hittite army of 2,500 chariots, and they met in battle at Qadesh. Rameses claimed a glorious victory in his bombastic records; and the Hittite records are remarkably silent about the outcome. It seems that the result was inconclusive, and the rivals recognised the necessity of ending a conflict that had proved unprofitable to both sides. Even before the Syrian campaign Muwatalli was engaged with the Arzawans, and in the face of increasing threats from the Kaska had felt obliged to move the capital to Tarhuntassa in the south, leaving his young and ambitious brother Hattusili as king in the north with a wide-ranging command against Kaska invasion.

Hattusili took over the throne in 1286 after a civil war, and ruled for twenty years as Hattusili III. Early in his reign the kingdom of Mitanni, a Hittite vassal, fell to the Assyrians, and in the face of this new threat from the east, Hattusili concluded a peace treaty with Egypt in 1284, which was cemented by the marriage of a Hittite princess to Rameses II in 1271. At home, Hattusili was involved in endless wars with the Kaska and Arzawa.

His son, Tudhaliya IV (c. 1265–1235) was probably the last Hittite ruler of any note. But now Hittite power was once again moving inexorably into decline. Under his son Arnuwanda III (c. 1235–1225) a widespread, serious famine occurred, and the Egyptian Pharaoh Merneptah sent grainships 'to keep alive the land of Hatti' in 1235. Three years later, famished Libyans attacked Egypt, reinforced by an alliance of northern seaborne forces which included peoples from Ahhiyawa (?) and Lukka in north-western Anatolia and the city of Tarsus in Kizzuwadna (Cilicia). It is possible that they had been driven out of their homelands by an invasion of famine-stricken Phrygians from Thrace onto the shores of the Sea of Marmara, although the evidence for this is admittedly controversial.

The final collapse of the Hittite New Kingdom soon after c. 1200 is usually blamed on the invasion of the so-called 'Sea-Peoples' who attacked Egypt in 1194 and were repulsed by Rameses III. Personally I do not agree with this interpretation; nor do I agree with some of the fanciful identifications of the Sea-Peoples that have been advanced in the past.

We have to piece together the end of the Hittites from a variety of sources. A Hittite text records that the last Hittite king, Suppiluliama II (c. 1225–1195) engaged in action across the Euphrates against the Assyrians. Another tablet found at Hattusa records that Alasiya (Cyprus) had either revolted or been taken by the Sea-Peoples, but that Suppiluliama defeated the Alasiyan navy in a sea-battle and retook the island.

Tablets from the great archives discovered at Ugarit (modern Ras Shamra on the Syrian coast) mention a famine in Hatti. Ugarit is asked to send 2,000 measures of grain from Mukish to Ura (Silifke) on the Cilician coast, a 'matter of life and death'. In another letter Hammurabi, the last king of Ugarit, wrote desperately to the king of Alasiya that his land is abandoned and defenceless because his army is with the Hittite king and his fleet in the land of Lukka. Transport is urgently required from Ugarit for the Hittite king and the royal family, somewhere on the south coast.

As invading forces marched east, Suppiluliama made a stand at Lawazantiya in eastern Cilicia at the foot of the Amanus range, was defeated and fled, probably to Carchemish. The invading armies crossed the Amanus and reached Mukish in the Plain of Antioch, and enemy ships, reinforced by deserters, plundered the coasts. Then darkness falls.

The Egyptian texts report: 'The foreign countries made a conspiracy in their islands (*or* The lands of the north were agitated). All at once the lands were removed and scattered in the fray. No land could stand before their arms, from Hatti, Aleppo, Carchemish, Arzawa and Alasiya on, being cut off [i.e. destroyed] at one time. A camp was set up in a place in Amurru. They desolated the people, and its land was like that which has never come into being. They were coming towards Egypt, while the flame was prepared before them.'

Thus wrote Rameses III, in the eighth year of his reign, 1194 BC. A great sea and land battle followed, in which the Egyptians claimed victory, depicted in great detail on Rameses III's mortuary temple at Medinet Habu.

The Egyptians called their enemies the Peoples of the Sea, and they have given the mythographers a field-day. According to the Egyptian texts, they consisted of 'Peleset, Tjekker, Sheklesh, Denyen and Weshesh lands united'.

Some of the identifications of these peoples have been ludicrously far-fetched. The Peleset (who later settled in Palestine and were known as the Philistines) have been equated with Cretans, Tjekker with Teucrians from Salamis, Sheklesh with Sicilians, Sherden with Sardinians, Denyen with Danaan Greeks, while the Weshesh have defeated all attempts at identification. Like some of the proposed identifications of the earlier Sea-Peoples who tried to invade Merneptah's Egypt with the Libyans, these suggestions are all designed to create the impression of some great confederacy of the Aegean nations descending upon the eastern Mediterranean

OPPOSITE
Relief of underworld
god in the form of a
sword plunging into
the ground from
Yazılıkaya.

coastline. I prefer to believe that, as with the earlier invasion, this was another outpouring from Anatolia: Peleset, Tjekker and Sheklesh, not mentioned as islanders, could be Lukka people from the Pamphylian area, whereas the Denyen and the unidentified Weshesh may be seafarers from Adaniya and some other city in Kizzuwadna (Cilicia). In other words, all of them are peoples from the south coast of Turkey, seafarers familiar with the eastern Mediterranean, and caught up in the famines of the end of the thirteenth century. There is no compelling evidence to look for more exotic origins, and nothing to suggest that they were Mycenaean Greeks, Cretans, or even Illyrians or other Balkan tribes, as has been proposed.

The idea that the Sea-Peoples alone were responsible for the destruction of the Hittite state seems to me most unlikely; they merely dealt with its Syrian possessions and Cyprus. The real battles must have taken place on the Anatolian plateau, and in the absence of any historical texts we are quite in the dark as to what happened. Three factors must be borne in mind: the evidence for famine from Hatti to Libya since 1235 BC; Arzawan and Kaskan threats to the Hittite state, always strong but potentially disastrous in famine conditions; and eloquent signs of Hittite weakness since the accession of Arnuwanda III c. 1235. In view of what is known of Hittite history, the accession of a new king always led to uprisings among the peoples on the Hittite periphery, and the extra factor of famine may have tipped the balance, even without a hypothetical Phrygian invasion from Europe on the southern shores of the Sea of Marmara.

To my mind the destruction of the Hittite homeland cannot be ascribed to Sea-Peoples or Phrygians, but is more likely the work of the Kaska, who were installed in central Hatti in the eighth century. The area from the Salt Lake to the Euphrates was taken over by East Luwian states, swamping any remnants of Hittites; and it is not impossible that what looks like a migration to the east started out as a traditional Arzawan conquest which led instead to the destruction of the Arzawa states as the Phrygian invasion hit them in the rear and carved a new homeland out of several Arzawa kingdoms. Rameses III reported the destruction of Arzawa as well as Hatti, information which was undoubtedly derived from prisoners. In the confusion of the twelfth to the tenth centuries BC, many adjustments of territories must have been made, and Mycenaean refugees from Greece managed to establish themselves on the western seaboard of Turkey from c. 1000 BC, meeting only local resistance. When Anatolia re-emerges into the dawn of recorded history in the early eighth century,

like Greece, the splendour and power of the Bronze Age was a thing of the past, dimly remembered and distorted beyond recognition by mythographers of new cities in search of a respectable ancestry.

Although the historical picture of the Hittite New Kingdom period is blurred and confused in places, fortunately the archaeological picture is infinitely clearer. Our main source is the excavations at Boğazköy, the Hittite capital, which has yielded an archive of 10,000 clay tablets which form the basis of our knowledge of Hittite history. Hattusa [Khatusha] has been excavated since 1906 by a German expedition led first by the Assyriologist H. Winckler and then by O. Puchstein, an architect, and since 1931 by the eminent archaeologist Kurt Bittel.

After the destruction of the capital by the Kaska around 1400 BC, it was probably the warrior king Suppiluliuma I (1380–1345) who conceived the grandiose reconstruction and the huge fortifications surrounding the upper city, which was eventually to cover 168 hectares, the largest Bronze Age site in Turkey and a fitting monument to Suppiluliuma's glory. The upper city had five gates; three of them were decorated with monumental sculptures—the King's Gate, Lion Gate and Sphinx Gate. In the warrior god on the King's Gate with his determined face one would like to see a portrait of the great king, but this sculpture is unfortunately uninscribed.

In the lower city near the Tawinian gate it may also have been Suppiluliuma who built an enormous temple of the Weather-god of Hatti, surrounded by massive magazines, priests' quarters and the ordinary houses of a busy lower city. The great temple with its huge foundations and several storeys in mud-brick dominates the lower city. Four other temples on a smaller scale were built during the fourteenth and thirteenth centuries BC in the upper city, but they have not yet been identified with various dates, and the builder or builders are unknown. All five temples show variations on a common plan: a monumental entrance leads into a paved and porticoed court, which may contain a small rectangular structure, variously interpreted as a place for libations or a tower for offerings. At the far end of the building, indirectly approached from the court is a *cella*, lit by windows, which contained a pedestal, probably for a statue of the god, although no trace of any has survived. Perhaps, as a set of texts tells us, they were made of various metals, bronze, silver, gold or iron, each deity with his appropriate symbolic animals and pedestals, which would have been carried off and melted down when the Hittite kingdom fell. Large stone statues are rare, and only one monumental

74

Gold pendant in the form of a goddess holding a child said to be from Kirşehir. Old Hittite period.

figure has survived on a hillside at Fasilar in western Anatolia, perhaps outside the Hittite frontier.

Such representations of Hittite deities in the round that have survived are small, 5–6 cms in height or even smaller, and often provided with a ring at the back to be worn as amulets. They are made of bronze, gold, rock crystal or ivory. The use of metal for the fashioning of statues of divinities dates back to the Early Bronze Age. It was not confined to the Hittites, and was to last into the Urartian period.

Fortunately the Hittites also carved figures of their deities on rocks; outside the gates of Hattusa lies the famous rock sanctuary of Yazılıkaya ('Inscribed rock'). It consists of an open area, closed from the profane gaze by a complicated temple structure, frequently remodelled, through which access was gained. On the rocks on either side two processions of gods, predominantly males on the left and females on the right, march towards the far end, corresponding to the *cella* in the temples, where the two meet in a larger than life-size scene, complete with sacred animals and symbols. Hieroglyphic inscriptions (a Luwian script) are here used in a Hittite sanctuary to represent a Hurrian pantheon led by the Weather-god Teshup, followed by the local Weather-god of Hatti on the left, to meet his wife Hepat and her son Sarruma on the right, each at the head of their own processions. It has been suggested that this sanctuary was used for the *purulliya* festival, the meeting of the gods on New Year's Day to bestow their blessings on the king and nation for the coming year. The much weathered reliefs, once probably stuccoed and painted, are still very impressive, but the air of sanctity is even stronger in a narrow side chamber. Near its entrance is a fine relief of King Tudhaliya IV, standing on mountains and probably deified. Lion-headed demons guard the narrow entrance facing a pedestal, perhaps of a statue of the same king. On one wall of the constricted passage that forms a chamber is carved a dagger with lions gripping the hilt from which a god's head emerges—probably a god of death. A row of figures on the opposite wall are interpreted as his attendants. Then follows a splendid relief of King Tudhaliya embraced by the god Sarruma. On the opposite wall empty niches are found, perhaps the final resting place for the cremated remains of Hittite kings. The dating of Yazılıkaya with its Hurrian pantheon falls clearly in the later thirteenth century, and most scholars would assign it to Tudhaliya IV, though others prefer his father Hattusili III and his Hurrian wife Puduhepa. The side chamber might actually be a funerary monument of Tudhaliya IV, added by his son Suppiluliama II, the last Hittite king, and possibly referred to in one of his texts.

Tudhaliya IV also reconstructed the interior of Hattusa's citadel on a large scale. An irregular space, measuring some 250 × 150 metres, was surrounded by massive foundations and rose in several tiers to the top of the rock where the king's residential palace is thought to have stood. Except for traces of a court with a colonnade and two cisterns, nothing now remains and any reconstruction is purely hypothetical. Probably two-storeyed, it would have commanded a splendid view of the city, the fields, forests and on the horizon to the north the Pontic Mountains, home of the Weather-god of Nerik.

The building stood in an upper court along two sides of which were long porticoes in front of two very important buildings, a huge audience hall supported by twenty-five columns and the main archive building, in which inscribed tablets were stacked like books on shelves, duly labelled and indexed. Beyond the audience hall there were two further buildings, residential or official, and a third outside the court was built on a bastion, which was added to the original design by one of Tudhaliya's sons. A columned propylon led down to a lower court with colonnades behind which further buildings were arranged; one of these bore traces of painting, and had a sacred pool behind it. A further building perched on the citadel wall faced the pool. On the opposite side of the court a propylon led to a ramp which gave access to a gate leading directly to the lower city. On either side were large buildings, some of which look like magazines. Behind them was a small structure in which a stela of Tudhaliya IV was discovered, perhaps a private shrine.

At the lower end of the paved court a series of rooms may have been occupied by the guards, and a simple gate and ramp led to a third triangular court facing a monumental gate with underground postern which led through the lower enceinte to the upper city. Next to it was another gate linking the two cities, bypassing the citadel. Most of the buildings on the citadel had more than one storey, but only the foundations have survived, so that restorations are somewhat uncertain. However, it would appear that not a few strongly resembled Hurrian buildings typical of north Syria (the so-called *bit-hilani*). In view of the Hurrianising tendencies of the Hittite court, especially since the reign of Hattusili III and his Hurrian wife Puduhepa, such influences are perhaps not surprising.

The recent excavation of a Hittite palace at Maşat Höyük a

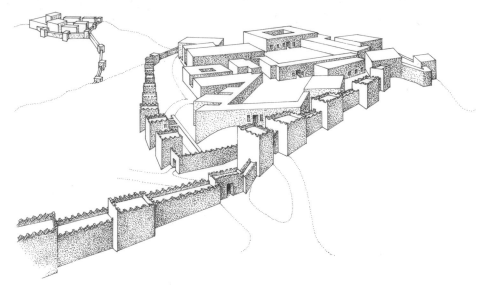

A reconstruction of the citadel of Hattusa in the thirteenth century BC.

hundred kilometres east of Hattusa by Professor T. Özgüc, associated with tablets of Tudhaliya III, may give us some idea of what earlier Hittite palaces were like, when published.

The thorough looting of Hittite sites at the time of the overthrow and the custom of cremating the dead has resulted in a dearth of small finds, in particular metalwork, vessels, weapons and jewellery, which are much better known in earlier periods. Most of the pottery found is clearly kitchen ware, coarse or plain and with a very restricted range of shapes. Pottery used for cultic purposes is altogether different with its splendid red and white burnished surfaces, and occasional painted, modelled or impressed designs. Fine libation jugs of Syrian type, censers and theriomorphic vessels in the shape of a pair of splendid bulls, lions, ducks or vessels with architectural detail such as towers show considerable artistic imagination. The texts show that iron was now used on a wider scale than before in the manufacture of sceptres and statuettes, jars, ornaments, and treaty-tablets, and in the decoration of thrones, doors, altars, and weapons such as daggers. In the past the Hittite use of iron has been exaggerated out of all proportion, and the idea that it was through a monopoly of iron-working that the Hittites were militarily superior is totally at variance with the evidence. Among the Hittites, as among their neighbours, bronze remained the essential metal, and safeguarding of supplies of tin a constant preoccupation.

# 7

# Mushku and Hatte: Phrygians and 'Neo-Hittites'

The catastrophe around 1200 BC in which all the Late Bronze Age kingdoms of Anatolia perished under the impact of the Phrygian and Kaskan invasions radically changed the map of what was to become Iron Age Anatolia. To foreign observers like the Assyrians or Urartians, however, the picture had not changed much, and they record the two main protagonists as 'Mushku' and 'Hatte'—in modern terminology, Phrygian and Neo-Hittites (also called Syro-Hittites, Neo-Luwians or East Luwians). In broad terms they were the successors of Arzawan and Hittite power. The Kaska, now peacefully installed in the Hittite homeland, had achieved their aims and thus ceased to be a menace, but a new turbulent element now appeared in the Antitaurus; this was the Hilakku, who were eventually to give their name to Cilicia. The Hurrians, once strong in the area, were now retrenched east of the Euphrates, where they had formed the powerful kingdom of Urartu *c.* 850 BC.

The eastward shift in power left a vacuum on the Aegean coast, where from *c.* 1050 BC onwards Mycenaean refugees from Greece established narrow footholds on the shorelands and on the adjacent islands which had once been held by Anatolian mainlanders. What they had failed to do in Mycenaean times, they achieved now; and gradually Greek colonies spread along the seaboard of Asia Minor, meeting little opposition. Nothing substantial has survived from the early stage of the Ionian cities but their pottery, known as protogeometric (*c.* 1050–900) and geometric (ninth and eighth centuries). Most of the settlers would have been refugees from Attica and the islands, poor men in a poor world, still suffering from the collapse of the Bronze Age.

In the northern mountains, tribes of Mysians, Bithynians and Paphlagonians (Balkan tribes like the Phrygians) established themselves and mixed with remnants of the Bronze Age population. The rugged Taurus Mountains of the south became a relict area for others who had lost their homes in the north, when the Phrygians crossed the Sea of Marmara and established themselves on the western Anatolian plateau: the Carians, Lycians, Pisidians and Pamphylians of classical times, who became archaeologically tangible from *c*. 700 BC, and were perhaps semi-nomadic before.

Archaeologically the break with the Late Bronze Age cultures is almost complete and in the greater part of Anatolia the Early Iron Age (*c*. 1200–850 BC) is a total blank, a real Dark Age. Almost, but not quite; for at a number of sites the Bronze Age culture lingered on into the twelfth and eleventh centuries, or reappeared somewhat altered in the ninth and eighth centuries, when a slow revival took place. The real strength of old tradition is shown in the language and religion, to which most people clung with great tenacity, however much the material culture changed and new ruling classes appeared—in Phrygia, for instance. The importance of a Bronze Age substratum in Iron Age cultures should not be underestimated, and in Anatolia it can be traced well into the late Classical period, in some places even into the Byzantine period.

The most obvious casualty of the collapse of the Bronze Age was literacy. This was only retained by the political heirs of the Hittites, the so-called Neo-Hittites or Syro-Hittite kingdoms which had been pushed back by Kaskan and Phrygian invasions to the eastern end of the Anatolian plateau, and the area between Antitaurus and the Euphrates with an extension into north Syria—the 'Hatte' of the Assyrian and Urartian texts. Supremely disunited, as might be expected in this mountainous terrain, the kingdoms of Tabal, Tuhana, Hilakku, Qu'e (Adana plain), Melid (Malatya), Kummuh, Gurgum, Patin and most powerful of all, Carchemish, still employed the old hieroglyphic script to write their monumental inscriptions in Luwian (cuneiform writing had perished in the 1200 upheaval). The use of the Luwian script and language shows clearly that we are not dealing with Hittites, but with their former Luwian subjects, people from the old kingdoms of Kizzuwadna, Tarhuntassa, or Arzawans from western Anatolia. It is for this reason that many archaeologists prefer the term 'Neo-Luwian' or East Luwian to Neo-Hittite or Syro-Hittite for these Iron Age cultures. The hated Hittite oppressors had gone, only to be replaced in due course by something worse, the

This costume from the Maraş area in Turkey still shows the influence of its East Luwian origins.

79

OPPOSITE
*Above* Urartian
wallpainting of calf
from Argisti I's palace
at Erebuni.

*Below* Lycian
dignitary, from a rock-
cut tomb at Karaburun
near Elmali.

Assyrians—a menace they faced bravely over the coming centuries.

Stimulated, one suspects, by Assyrian victory accounts, the Urartians from *c.* 850 BC also revived literacy in their own Hurrian language. In the west of Anatolia, however, writing in cuneiform and hieroglyphics died *c.* 1200 BC; and when the need for recording reappeared in eighth-century western Anatolia and Greece, it was neither cuneiform nor hieroglyphic that was revived but a new alphabetic script devised by the Phoenicians. Phrygian, Carian, Lydian, Lycian and Greek all adopted the Phoenician script with individual variations, and in the present stage of our knowledge it is hard to say who came first; perhaps it was the Phrygians, the most powerful of the kingdoms, whose king, Mita, is recorded in Assyrian texts as interfering in the affairs of Cilicia in 717 BC. This was a region where the Phoenician script was already known and used for monumental inscriptions in the eighth century BC at the famous site of Karatepe. The establishment of a Greek colony at Al Mina, at the mouth of the Orontes, however, allows for an independent borrowing of the Phoenician alphabet, without intermediaries.

The most immediate effect of restricted literacy during the Iron Age is to deprive us of any historical information other than that supplied by the enemy, the Assyrians. Urartu forms the only exception, for the Luwian hieroglyphics only record religious foundations of no immediate historical interest barring a few items of royal genealogy. The very few Phrygian, Lydian, Carian and Lycian inscriptions are equally devoid of historical content; yet all hope should not be lost, for there are indications that writing on other materials than stone (lead and wax, for instance) was practised, and more examples of these may well come to light in future excavations. Suffice it to say that the Assyrian records, combined with the Luwian hieroglyphic inscriptions enable the historian to set up a rough chronology and at least a general picture of the political geography of the time. Little as that may be, such information is lacking in western Anatolia and we know of only one Phrygian king, Mita of Mushku. With so little help from the texts, our knowledge of the Iron Age cultures of Anatolia is essentially derived from excavations; hence it is very uneven and much in need of improvement, especially in East Luwian states, which have not received the attention they deserve.

The major example of a city built by the East Luwians is Carchemish, which lies on the west bank of the Euphrates on the frontier with Syria. It was partially excavated by Sir Leonard Woolley before the First World War. The Iron Age city has a citadel, an inner

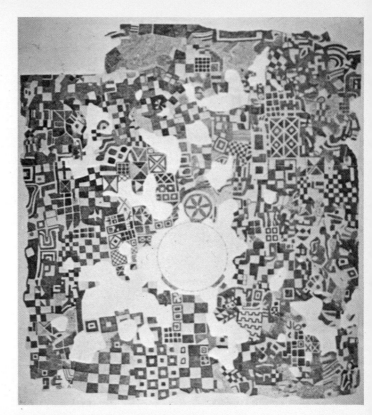

city with temples and an outer city all surrounded with strong walls and gates. Carchemish was already an important city in the Bronze Age, and under Suppiluliuma it became the seat of the Hittite viceroy of Syria until it was destroyed *c*. 1200 BC; but unlike most Hittite sites it was probably soon rebuilt by the new Luwian royal house that established an important kingdom here still called 'Great Hatte' by the Assyrians, who had traditionally coveted its possession ever since its capture by the Hittites from Mitanni in 1352 BC. Carchemish remained a thorn in the Assyrian side until its last king, Pisiris, who was plotting an alliance with Midas of Phrygia, was deposed by Sargon in 717 BC and incorporated into the Assyrian Empire. From *c*. 1000–717 BC various Luwian dynasties ruled Carchemish and left many statues, reliefs and inscriptions, but with the exception of the walls, a number of gates and the courtyard walls and entrance to a temple of the Weather-god of Carchemish, little is known of the buildings of the city. Woolley's dig was interrupted by the First World War, and the actual temple or temple complex, and the citadel, which would have contained the palaces, still await excavation.

There is, however, another city of this period, Zincirli (ancient Sam'al) at the foot of the Amanus Mountains opposite the Bahce pass, which was excavated by a German expedition under F. von Luschan. Although built for an Aramaean dynasty around 900 BC, the architects may have come from neighbouring Carchemish. A perfectly circular wall (doubled in Assyrian times), 720 metres in diameter, was studded with one hundred towers and pierced by three equidistant gates. The south gate, facing the kingdom of Patin in the plain of Antioch, gave access to a citadel built on an earlier mound in the centre of the city; this citadel was also surrounded by a wall with towers but with only a single gate. The citadel is divided by further walls and gates into four sections at different levels. To the east it contained rooms for a garrison, and on the highest north-western part lay a palace with separate summer and winter quarters, each arranged on one side of a colonnaded courtyard. These main buildings are of Hurrian *hilani* type, a tripartite structure with a portico with two or three columns, in front of which lies a broad flight of steps, with a bastion at one corner. Behind the portico are two long rooms transversely placed which give access to smaller rooms. The persistence of Late Bronze Age Hurrian features into the Iron Age therefore presents problems as to what constitutes East Luwian architecture.

More western, perhaps, is an eighth-century temple of megaron

*Above* Transcript of the mosaic below.

*Below* Pebble mosaic in one of the smaller megarons in Gordion from the eighth century BC.

King Yariris of
Carchemish with his
son.

shape at Tell Tainat in the Amuq, just across the road from Alalakh,
which can possibly be equated with Kinalua, the capital of the
kingdom of Patin. This is quite different from the late Bronze Age
temples at Alalakh, or the richly decorated tenth-century temple at
Ain Dara not far away. What should be borne in mind is that the
Luwians, as newcomers in north Syria, found strongly entrenched
local Bronze Age traditions, Semitic, Hurrian and Hittite, and with so
little excavation it is perhaps not surprising that the modern
archaeologist is somewhat bewildered.

Not far away on the Seyhan River lies Karatepe (Azitawandiya) a
short-lived summer palace of the kings of the Adana plain, which was

excavated by a Turkish expedition under H. Bossert, Halet Çambel and Bahadir Alkim. Karatepe is chiefly famous for its bilingual inscriptions in Luwian hieroglyphs and Phoenician, which led to the decipherment of the hieroglyphs. The date of this fortress, perched on a rock with a splendid view of the Amanus and the forested hills of the Antitaurus, can be deduced from the fact that its builder, Azitawandas, was favoured by Awarikus, king of Adana, who appears under the name of Urikki in the Assyrian records between 738 and 709 BC. The building on the top of the rock is in ruins but it seems to be of the same *hilani* plan. The famous reliefs and inscriptions are found on two great gates in the wall that surrounds the site. Although the contents of these reliefs are fascinating, informative, and sometimes humorous, their artistic standard reaches an all-time low, bordering on the grotesque. Many of the scenes were unfinished when the fortress was burnt. One hates to think what these sculptures might have been like when finished and painted!

The study of East Luwian archaeology is dominated by relief-decorated and inscribed orthostats carved in basalt or limestone, which graced city and palace gates, entrances to temple precincts, temple podia and column and statue bases. A small number of monumental sculptures in the round representing deities and kings have been found. With very rare exceptions this large body of sculpture dates from between *c*. 930–700 BC. The subject matter of these sculptures is predominantly religious; the king and his family, army and subjects in procession to honour the gods of Carchemish; a

Children of King
Yariris of Carchemish.

triad consisting of Tarhundas, the Weather-god, Kupapa, his wife and protectress of the city, and their son (?) Karhuhas, a god of war; and so on. Occasionally mythological scenes and libations to the gods were carved, as on the gate of Malatya. Myths, feasting and jollity occur on the 'Heralds' wall' at Carchemish and at Karatepe. Historical events do not seem to have been portrayed, and Suhis II's procession of chariots, trampling victims, or his inscription framed by human heads and hands may symbolise royal power rather than signify a specific event. The reliefs of King Yariris (c. 800) and his family on the 'Royal buttress' at Carchemish are among the most accomplished carvings and introduce some charming details like his children with their spinning tops and pet animals.

The information that can be gleaned from East Luwian sculpture is of great importance in that it tells us much about dress, coiffure, armament, etc. that could not survive the ravages of time. Evidence for cultural influence from the East Luwian world on its neighbours is starting to accumulate. Their sculpture influenced the naturalistic animal style of eighth-century Phrygian pottery, and the splendid stone reliefs from Ankara with bull, lion and sphinx are clearly derived from East Luwian sculpture.

Unlike the Urartians and East Luwians, who were natives of Anatolia, the third main ethnic power of the Anatolian Iron Age, the Phrygians, were foreigners from south-east Europe. By the period c. 800 BC, however, when they emerge from obscurity, their culture had become almost as distinctly Anatolian as that of their neighbours. Famous in antiquity, the rediscovery of the Phrygians is mainly due to the late Rodney S. Young of the University of Pennsylvania through his conscientious and systematic excavations of Gordion, the Phrygian capital, from 1950 to his tragic death in 1974. Gordion is a lasting memorial to this great archaeologist.

The citadel of Gordion lay on an ancient mound, called Yassı Hüyük in Turkish, ninety kilometres west of Ankara on the banks of the River Sakarya. It covered some twenty acres and was surrounded by a strong wall of stone masonry still thirteen metres high and with a gate passage on the east facing the cemetery and approached by a narrow ramp. The gate gave access to a series of paved courts around which about ten important buildings of a palace complex were erected, each freestanding, of megaron plan, facing the court. The largest and oldest of these, dated to c. 760 BC, was originally set within its own enclosure wall and consisted of a great hall, 20 by 16 metres surrounded on three sides by a wooden gallery supported by two rows

The great royal tumulus of Gordion.

of four wooden posts. The gallery was used for storage or for occupations like weaving. A hearth probably occupied the centre of the room and in front of it lay a wide vestibule or entrance room. The walls were of mud-brick on high stone foundations and contained a plastered-over timber framework, and they were covered with a low gabled roof of wood, reeds and clay, crowned with a carved stone acroterion. The other structures were essentially of the same type, but some had hearths also in the ante-room and several had geometrically patterned mosaic floors of black, red and white pebbles, perhaps in imitation of the floor cover of the great megaron which had no mosaics and might have been covered with rugs laid on felt.

How these buildings were decorated we do not know, but there are remains of snarling lions' and bulls' heads carved in soft limestone, probably painted, unfortunately no longer *in situ*. Of wallpaintings there is no trace, but much of the woodwork could have been carved. Colourful textile hangings may have decorated these halls, and fragments of furniture were found in the great hall, including scenes of herdsmen driving a row of cattle set between exquisite geometric borders, as well as ivory furniture inlays.

Huge craters over one metre in height and width and decorated with animal figures in a style derived from East Luwian sculpture may have been standing in some of these buildings when the city was burned by the Cimmerian hordes *c*. 696 BC. Fortunately a series of intact tombs of the late eighth to early seventh centuries have preserved wooden furniture of the type burnt by the invaders: great wooden screens inlaid in a variety of woods with striking geometric patterns and roundels with curvilinear design of Late Bronze Age descent, as well as a variety of tables on three or four feet and

85

Reconstruction of the
great megaron at
Gordion.

with remarkable openwork carving. The discovery of elaborate
wooden furniture is of great importance as it has long been surmised
that western Anatolia, rich in forests and blatantly averse to stone
sculpture in the Bronze Age, might have exercised its artistic skills on
other materials of which wood and textiles, both perishable, are the
most obvious.

Behind the row of great megara lay terraces, one of which carried
two rows of eight to nine buildings, over a hundred metres long,
facing each other along a street which may have led to a water gate in
the west wall and a bridge across the river. Each individual unit is
again of megaron type, but the outer room with its hearth, oven and
horseshoe-shaped cooker, was probably partly open to the sky. The
inner rooms were provided with a gallery along three sides and some
had grinding platforms large enough to provide working space for six
people. Some of these buildings seem purely domestic and they were
probably palace kitchens and workshops for weavers; others may
have accommodated a garrison.

Gordion's cemetery contained seventy-six tumuli (grave mounds),
just about the largest concentration on any Iron Age site in Turkey.
Of these, six pre-Cimmerian tombs, including four of the largest,
have been investigated and found to belong to the second half of the
eighth century, the climax of Phrygian culture, and the period of the
main buildings on the mound. At this time the dead were buried in a
doorless gabled chamber, the replica of a house. Placed off-centre to
deter robbers, tons of rubble were piled over the wooden tomb to
form a mound. This was covered with an impervious layer of clay to
prevent damp getting in, and on top of this clay layer, which is still
intact in many tombs, the bulk of an earthen tumulus was piled to a
height of up to sixty metres. These tumuli, a Phrygian import from
Europe and unknown before in Anatolia, contain individual burials,
though on occasion a pair of horses may have been buried with the
dead. For secondary burials elsewhere in the tumulus there is no
evidence and the practice of cremation burial under tumuli does not
appear at Gordion until after the Cimmerian destruction, i.e. in the
seventh century BC, the Lydian period (cf. chapter 9).

In the Great Tomb of Gordion, the body of a rather short man
about sixty-five years old was found lying on his back on a wooden
bed, covered with felt and layer upon layer of richly patterned woollen
and linen textiles. Near him lay a bag with nearly two hundred bronze
*fibulae* (ornamental safety-pins) which were worn with the bow
hanging down as shown on Warpalawa's relief at Ivriz. These appear

to be a Phrygian invention. Bronze drinking vessels such as omphalos bowls, plain, ringed or petalled like the lotus flower they imitate, trefoil-mouthed and plain jugs, ladles and bowls with ring handles totalled another 150 items. Three of these ring-handled bowls bore Phrygian inscriptions on a strip of beeswax, which remain undeciphered. Among the more special objects found in the tomb were two fine buckets, one with a ram's, the other with a lion's head, interpreted as of Urartian or Assyrian origin or inspiration. Then there were three great bronze cauldrons on iron stands; one was plain, the second had two male and two female handle attachments, whereas on the third these were in the form of winged females or sirens. Opinions are divided about the origin of these cauldrons. Some

Ivriz relief of King
Warpalawa, King of
Tyana, wearing
Phrygian dress.

regard them as Urartian, others favour an East Luwian origin for those with sirens, still others maintain a Phrygian origin copying imports. Fragments of yet another cauldron type with griffin heads came from the great hall, and to scoop the liquid out of these great vessels ladles were used, one ornate example ending in a duck's head.

There are a number of unusual features that strike one about this undoubtedly royal tomb, reliably dated to *c.* 725 BC. First of all is the absence of any identification of the king. It can hardly be King Midas himself, who figures in Assyrian records of 717, 715 and 709, too late to be the Great Tomb's occupant; but perhaps it was his father Gordias, a semi-legendary figure, reputedly the founder of Gordion and owner of the famous knot on the chariot pole, whose unravelling promised the rule of Asia to whoever accomplished it — a prophecy that came true when Alexander the Great sliced through it with his sword. Secondly one is surprised by the absence of weapons, jewellery or any precious object in gold, silver, electrum, ivory, glass or faience, and by the lack of any object of a clearly religious nature. This austerity, equally manifest in the other excavated tombs of this period, might have been a Phrygian custom but it certainly is disappointing in view of the Greek legends about King Midas's golden touch and immense wealth.

Numerous other finds from tombs and burned buildings bear witness to Phrygian prosperity. From the tomb of a young prince come three engraved bronze belts, a fluted clear glass bowl (similar to an Assyrian one with the name of Sargon), probably an import, a set of wooden toy animals and a number of gaily painted pots, including two in the form of geese. Phrygian pottery consists of monochrome grey ware, which clearly had its origins in the Late Bronze Age pottery of north-west Anatolia, and a much rarer painted and burnished ware with brown to black designs on a cream or buff ground bearing panels with bulls, deer, hawks, lions and a sphinx derived from East Luwian carvings in a geometric framework like that found on woodwork and textiles. Many of the pottery vessels are imitations of the bronzes and as before micaceous washes are used on monochrome ware to copy a metal sheen.

Although there is a considerable amount of imported pottery, there are no Greek imports; these did not appear until much later, *c.* 650–640 BC. In the eighth century the awakening Greek world was not yet in a position to influence Phrygia; rather it was the other way round. Phrygian exports were much appreciated and spread wide and far throughout Greece, especially metalwork: cauldrons, omphalos

Bronze lion bucket from the Royal Tomb at Gordion.

bowls, ring-handled bowls, *fibulae* and probably also textiles and furniture. Perhaps the Phrygian alphabet influenced writing among the early Greeks; a peculiar Phrygian sign, called *sampi*, used to write -ss- and unknown to the Greek alphabet, is used in Greek cities from Halikarnassos to the Black Sea. Phrygian caps and Phrygian music were admired in Greece, just as *bouzouki* music is today.

At the height of their power the Phrygians probably controlled the greater part of the west Anatolian plateau from the mouth of the Halys to the Taurus Mountains, perhaps with vassal states in Lydia, in the south-west and in the north, territories which surrounded the Phrygian homeland. Overland trade routes linked Phrygia with east and west alike, precursors of the Persian Royal Road and it was no doubt the lure of the East that drew Midas, like Hittite kings and Luwians before him, to conquest in Cilicia and an alliance with Pisiris, the last king of Carchemish against Sargonid encroachment. Eloquent evidence of such an '*Ost-Politik*' is found in Assyrian texts and exemplified by exotic imports at Gordion; glass vessels, linen cloth or garments and North Syrian ivories in the form of horse trappings, frontlets and cheek pieces as well as iron snaffle bits (conceivably a royal gift of a chariot team) and the cauldrons with iron tripods of the splendid *situlae*, from the great royal tomb.

The Phrygian economy is still little known, but agriculture must

Bronze bowl with strip of beeswax bearing Phrygian inscription from the Royal Tomb at Gordion.

have formed the basis, with widespread stock breeding. Horses were bred for cavalry and chariotry, sheep for the Phrygian wool industry and a graffito on a wall leading to an outdoor lavatory shows that most ferocious of Anatolian animals, the *kocabaş* ('big-head') sheepdog with a spiked collar as a protection against wolves. Cattle and herdsmen are shown on a fragment of furniture and camel bones have been found. Among the pottery and metalwork there are goats, geese and ducks, probably domestic, and a familiar sight in the villages as today. The presence of lions and birds of prey in Phrygian art reminds one of the attributes of the chief goddess Kybele whose chariot was reputedly drawn by lions, but Phrygian religion is one of the subjects on which the otherwise rich information from Gordion has as yet failed to throw any light. Until this happens one is justified in treating the late classical accounts of Phrygian religion, with its excessive celebrations so alien to Anatolia, with caution if not scepticism.

# 8

# Urartu

Of all the Anatolian kingdoms of the Iron Age the most powerful was Urartu, although for most of its existence it was locked in mortal combat with its formidable southern neighbour, Assyria. Although Urartu ('land of Ararat') occurs as a geographical term as early as the thirteenth century, the Assyrians from the time of Tiglath-Pileser I in the late twelfth century referred to their neighbour as 'Nairi'. By 850 BC, Urartu was already a strong kingdom, apparently formed from a loose confederation and led by King Arame; the Assyrian King Shalmaneser III then destroyed its capital, Arzaskun, an event depicted on the Balawat gates in the British Museum. Arzaskun has not yet been located, but it is thought to lie near the north-western corner of Lake Van, where Tiglath-Pileser had also set up his victory stele at Bulanik.

After Shalmaneser's campaign, Urartu gradually rose to pro-minence as Assyrian might declined. The earliest inscriptions, which were written in Assyrian cuneiform, come from Arame's successor, Sardur I, who may have been the first to choose the rock of Van as his capital, Tushpa, further away from the threat of Assyrian attack — though we hear that Shalmaneser III also attacked him there in 835 BC.

Under Sardur's successor, Ishpuini, we find the first texts written in Urartian (a Hurrian language but in Assyrian cuneiform script); but all Urartian monumental inscriptions are disappointingly laconic, and fuller records written on other materials such as clay have not yet been found. The history of Urartu depends mainly on Assyrian references to it, and secondly on native records which yield precious information for campaigns and building works in territories beyond the ken of

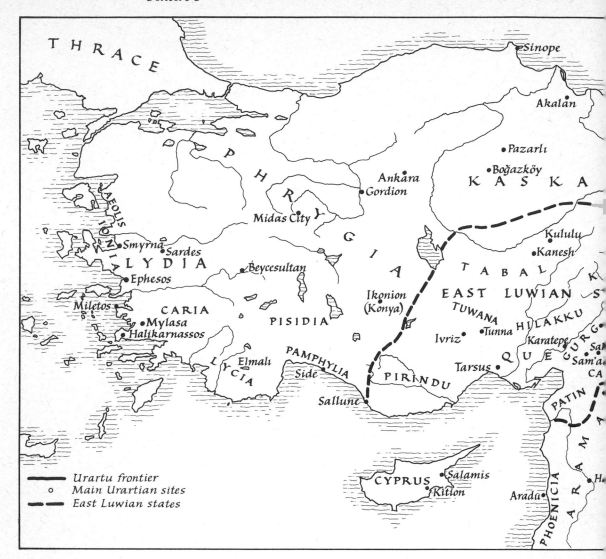

The Iron Age.

Assyrian scribes. From these records we can piece together some idea of the growth and subsequent decline of Urartu between 856 and *c*. 600, when it disappeared as an independent state and was swallowed up by the Medes soon after they had destroyed its great rival Assyria in 612 BC.

Under Ishpuini, Urartu already extended from Lake Van to Lake Urmia (Rezayyieh) 'from the Upper to the Lower Sea of Nairi', whereas to the south of Lake Urmia the Urartian hegemony extended over Mannea and Parsua, thereby forming a threat to Assyria proper from the region of Zamua (Suleymania in Iraqi Kurdistan). The Assyrian king claimed to have taken eleven cities and 200 villages

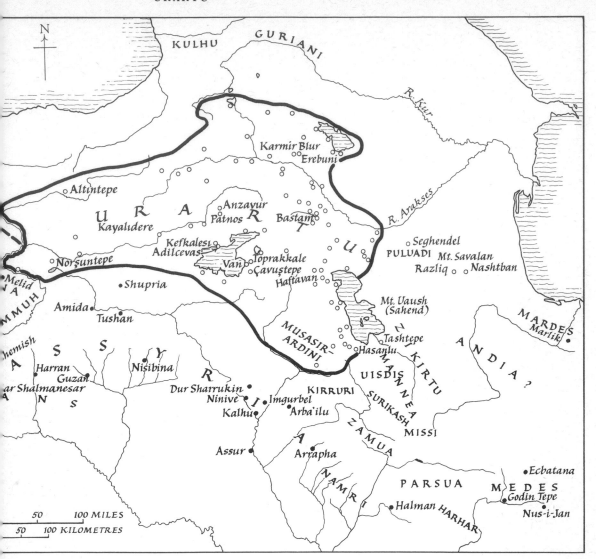

from 'Ushpina' and to have campaigned again the following year in 'Mannea' and 'Parsua'. The Manneans are thought to have been another Hurrian people, recorded in the area since the days of the Third Dynasty of Ur (2250–2143 BC), but 'Parsua' possibly refers to Persians, located north-west of Kermanshah on the age-old trade route from Babylonia to Iran; any Urartian attempt to gain influence in this area and control the trade route would have had the effect of cutting off Assyria's supply of horses from the Median steppe.

However that may be, the area figures prominently in Urartian records through the reigns of five successive kings until it was wrested from Urartu by Sargon II of Assyria in his famous eighth campaign of

714. The frontier of Urartu proper lay further north in Ardini (Musasir), probably in the mountain district of Hakkiari around the mighty peaks of Cilo Dağ (4,168 metres), the only mountain in the Taurus with a permanent glacier. Ardini commanded the Kel-i-Shin pass running from Assyria to the Ushnu valley on the Iranian plateau, where Urartian settlements begin. This pass appears to have been permanently blocked to the Assyrians, who thus had to enter Urartu through the Zagros (Mannea) and by Lake Urmia, as Sargon did in 714, or else go to the other end of Urartu and march first to Malatya on the Euphrates and then penetrate up the southern branch, the Murad Su, as Tiglath-Pileser I and Shalmaneser had done, and Tiglath-Pileser III was to do again in 735; a frontal attack from Assyria on Urartu was made impossible by the barrier of the Taurus Mountains, of which Ardini formed the eastern bulwark.

Ispuini's successor was his son Menua (810–786), probably Urartu's greatest king. He consolidated his father's kingdom and built fortresses to command the roads leading to Van, improving on his father's constructions by introducing regularly spaced rectangular towers along the curtain walls. If Ispuini's main concern had been with the Assyrian frontier, Menua's conquests expanded the kingdom in all other directions; into the fertile Araxes valley (Werakhram) around Mount Ararat, into the Erzerum plain, where he defeated the king of Diauehi at Hasankale, and to the west, down the Murat Su, where he made the Euphrates the frontier and exacted tribute from Suliehauli, the 'Neo-Hittite' king of Malatya. After 796 Assyrian influence in North Syria waned for a time, and Menua extended his hegemony south-westwards across the Euphrates as far as Patina (frequently misread as Hattina) in the Amuq plain, which gave Urartu access to the Mediterranean; not until 743 would Assyrian supremacy be restored with the defeat of Menua's grandson at Halpa in Kummuhi by Tiglath-Pileser III. For fifty years the Urartians lorded it over north Syria and this is reflected in the splendid Urartian griffin-headed cauldron found at Salamis in Cyprus, and perhaps also in the Urartian metalwork that reached Olympia and Etruria.

Apart from his warlike exploits, Menua was a great builder of fortress towns and canals for irrigation. His annals were found at Anzavur near Patnos, engraved on the walls of a typical square towerlike Urartian temple, with a single *cella* and buttresses at each corner; whereas those of his son and successor, Argishti I (786–764), were found carved on the walls of his rock-cut tomb on the great rock of Tushpa (Van).

94

Reconstruction of royal hunting scene from Argishti I's palace at Erebuni.

Argishti inherited a powerful kingdom and maintained it. He finally incorporated the Erzerum region into his domains and extended Urartian power into Transcaucasia, onto the shores of Lake Sevan, subduing the Etiu. He built fortresses, known as Argishtihinili (called after himself, a normal Urartian custom) at Armavir in the Ararat plain; he constructed canals, and he used deported slave labour from Hatti and Supani (the region of Malatya and Elazig) to construct a magnificent winter palace at Erebuni (Erevan) facing Ararat, decorated with wallpaintings. He also campaigned extensively in Mannea.

Urartian power and prosperity continued under his son Sardur II (764–735). The annals of his reign were inscribed on two stelae set up in an open sanctuary at the northern slope of Van, and new fortresses were built at Çavuştepe on the road to Hakkiari and at Kayalıdere on the Murad Su. The Lake Sevan region saw further conquests, and Qulha is mentioned as a new acquisition; possibly Sardur penetrated into Colchis, at the foot of the Caucasus. During the last ten years of his reign, however, events took a turn for the worse, for the long period of Assyrian inactivity was halted by the accession of Tiglath-Pileser III (745–727) who revived Assyrian aggression towards north Syria, which was still under Urartian

95

hegemony at this time. After conquering the Aramaean stronghold of Arpad near Aleppo, Tiglath-Pileser III met Sardur II in battle at Halpa in Kummuh in 743 and totally routed the Urartian and his allies. Northern Syria was thereby lost.

Eight years later, Tiglath-Pileser III penetrated right into the heart of Urartu in the first year of Rusa I (735–714). His siege of the capital was unsuccessful and Urartu survived the attack; and Rusa actually completed the conquest of the Sevan area, twenty-three districts paying tribute to him. The frontiers of Urartu were thus extended to the Little Caucasus, and the land of Guriana (probably the Kur valley around Tiflis) into which the Cimmerians had settled, paid tribute to him. According to Herodotus, these nomadic warriors from Southern Russia (the Crimea is still named after them) had been driven out of their territories by their eastern enemies, the Scythians. They crossed the Caucasus and thus escaped, and by 735 they are first attested in an Assyrian intelligence report. Further south more trouble was brewing: the Medes of western Iran were growing in strength and meddling in the affairs of Mannea, the disputed territory over which both Urartu and Assyria claimed suzerainty.

The accession of a powerful Assyrian king, Sargon II (721–705) brought matters to a head. In 719 Rusa instigated a Mannean revolt against the Assyrians, in 716 the Assyrians were fighting in Mannea, in 715 they were engaged with the Medes, and in 714 Sargon invaded Urartu in his eighth campaign. Assyrian intelligence was evidently good, for three Urartian army commanders, who had perhaps been invading Cimmerian territory, had already been defeated, and Rusa was thus faced with war on two fronts; in the Cimmerian counter-attack, several important Urartian strongholds were apparently taken and burned, among them Erebuni in the fertile Ararat plain and possibly even the palace of Giriktepe, just north of Lake Van. The barbarian Cimmerian inroads must have been a shattering blow to Urartian prestige; and it was at this point that Sargon decided to attack. Marching through Mannea by the familiar southern road through Zamua (Suleymaniye), he caught Rusa and his Mannean (or Median) allies unawares before they had time to deploy their forces at Mount Uaush (possibly Sahend, south of Tabriz). The Urartians were defeated and retreated, followed by Sargon who methodically laid waste the Urartian territory through which he passed. Skirting Lake Urmia from the north-east, Sargon passed through the mountains, reaching Lake Van at its eastern tip, and proceeded along its northern shore, and then probably traversed the Bitlis Pass through the Taurus. But before returning home he made a successful attack on Musasir-Ardini, where he plundered the temple of Haldi in this most holy city of the Urartians. This was the most shattering blow Urartu had ever received at the hands of the Assyrians. Eighty-seven cities were destroyed, according to Sargon, and though Urartu recovered, its great days were over. Never again did Urartu challenge the Assyrians, and it may be assumed that it was the threat of the Cimmerians that lay at the back of this.

From the Assyrian point of view, Urartu, once a mortal enemy, had become a most convenient buffer against the Cimmerians. Others too were aware of the danger; in 716 Mita of Mushki (probably the legendary king Midas of the Phrygians), whose territorial expansion

Urartian cauldron
found at Salamis in
Cyprus.

Bronze plaque with
Urartian rider.

towards Cilicia was causing concern in Assyria, offered to pay tribute
to Sargon and hand over Cilician envoys to Urartu, a gesture which
would have been somewhat inexplicable had there not been a looming
threat of Cimmerian attack. If Mita foresaw what was to come he
must have been well informed, for the Cimmerians who had attacked
Urartu in 714 came again in 706; this time they killed Sargon of
Assyria in battle somewhere in Anatolia in 705 and then burst into
central Anatolia. Sinop was destroyed *c.* 700, the Phrygian capital,
Gordion, went up in flames soon after 700 (696?) and in 652 Gyges,
King of Lydia, was slain in battle by the Cimmerians who reached the
Aegean, where they were recorded on painted Clazomenean
sarcophagi. The Cimmerian danger was not removed until 637–627
when Alyattes of Lydia defeated and expelled them, and they
abandoned the west and peacefully settled in Cappadocia (Gimir).

Neither the Cimmerian attacks nor Sargon's humiliating foray
broke Urartian resilience, though their power may have been curbed
and their domain diminished. Rusa I's successor, Argishti II
(714–685), built Altıntepe near Erzincan, possibly as a fort against the
Cimmerians; it was the north-westernmost Urartian stronghold,
with a temple, an audience hall with wallpaintings, an open-air shrine
and stone-built tombs with stone sarcophagi, some of which were
found, unplundered, by Tahsin and Nimet Özgüç of Ankara
University in a highly successful excavation. Argishti campaigned
even further east than any of his predecessors in the region east of
Tabriz, round Ahar and Ardebil, extending Urartian control almost
up to the Caspian.

The recovery of Urartu, now that peace reigned with Assyria, is
perhaps not surprising, as the forces of the kingdom would have been
quite strong enough to deal with any northern enemies. In the reign of
Rusa II (685–645) we see in fact a Urartian renaissance and important
building activities; two fortresses with their lower cities (both called
Rusahinili in the usual manner) were built, one at Bastam in north-
western Iran and the other at Toprakkale near Van as a new capital.
In the Araxes valley a mighty fortress called Teishebaini (Karmir
Blur) replaced the earlier capital of Erebuni which had been burnt by
the Cimmerians. Another great fortress and temple were built on
Lake Van at Kefkalesi and Adilcevas, with fine monumental sculpture.

After 645, however, Urartian power declined under its last three
kings, Sardur III, Erimena, and Rusa III (*c.* 625–585), who
recognised Assyria as overlord—evidently a sign of extreme crisis
caused by Scythian attacks on Karmir Blur. Perhaps the Medes were

already on the warpath; they destroyed Assyria for ever in 614–12, and Urartu itself was probably absorbed soon after 600 BC. In 585 Cyaxares, King of Media, fought a battle with Alyattes of Lydia on the Halys when there was an eclipse of the sun, and a treaty was made dividing Anatolia in half. In 547 Cyrus of Persia completed the conquest of Anatolia; the period of native Anatolian rule was over.

The aptly named Iron Age was not a time in which open settlements and rural towns flourished in the fertile plains; the great forts and fortified cities were strategically placed on sharp and pointed ridges, crowned with citadels at the foot of which nestled 'lower towns' protected by further curtain walls. In time of war the rural population could take refuge in these 'lower towns' with their herds and possessions, leaving their homes and crops to be burnt and their orchards cut down by a punitive enemy. The records of the Neo-Assyrian kings bear ample witness to man's inhumanity to man, and one may presume that the nomadic hordes of Cimmerian and Scythian horsemen were not exactly renowned for their gentleness either. How the Urartians countered such ferocity we do not know; like the Assyrians they themselves practised deportation, and one suspects that Assyrians in general preferred to avoid being taken prisoner. The extremely mountainous terrain favoured the Urartians, and certainly no king of theirs was ever captured by the Assyrians, nor as far as we know were any killed in battle.

An Urartian fortress contained a temple, usually square in plan with four towers at the corners, approached by a few steps and sometimes surrounded by a colonnaded court. In the *cella* stood a bronze statue of the deity, though none have survived, and in the courtyard a cauldron was placed on a tripod with bull's hoofs. Ceremonial spears and shields were fixed at the entrance and hung from the walls. The interior might be painted with scenes on a lapis lazuli blue background, or the doorway may have been carved with painted reliefs as in the fragments of a Teisheba temple at Adilcevas on Lake Van. The lower part of the walls consisted of fine ashlar masonry in basalt or limestone, whereas the superstructure was of plastered mud-brick. The towered square temple was the most common though not the only type; at Erebuni the temple is oblong, and the temple of Haldi at Ardini (Musasir) shown on a relief of Sargon II at Khorsabad shows yet a third type, a lower structure with two pillars *in antis*, and a low gabled roof.

We are ill informed about Urartian religion. The main god was evidently Haldi the War-god, invoked by kings in their victory

Reconstruction of the Altintepe temple.

inscriptions, whose symbol was a spear and who is shown as standing on a lion. Teisheba, the old Hurrian Weather-god standing on a bull, is also a prominent figure and there was a Sun-god, Shivini, who is somewhat more nebulous, usually shown supporting a sun-disc. His wife, Tushpuea, may be represented by the winged goddess who figures so prominently on the Urartian cult cauldrons. A god with a sun-disc shaped body standing on a winged horse supporting a crescent may have been a Moon-god. The winged griffins have as yet no owner, and apart from the three main deities there must have been many others in the Urartian pantheon, of whom little but the name is known, like Bagmashtu, the wife of Haldi, Irmusi and many others.

The second feature of the typical Urartian fortress was a columned hall, already found in thirteenth-century Hattusa and a regular feature also of Median and Achaemenian architecture, the *apadana*. Wooden columns were set on stone bases and such halls might be at ground level or even in a second storey. At Erebuni and Altintepe polychrome wallpaintings were found with rows of Assyrianised bulls and rosettes, friezes of genii carrying *situlae* (buckets) for watering stylised trees of life, as well as proper Urartian subjects such as royal hunting scenes with delightfully naturalistic animals. Unfortunately, only fragments have survived.

Besides the great audience halls, the palaces must have had private

apartments, probably on upper floors above rows and rows of
magazines containing huge pithoi for the storage of grain, oil, wine,
beer, etc., whose contents or capacity were marked in pictographs on
the rims of the pots. Other rooms contained crockery, weapons (iron
swords, and bows and arrows), bronze quivers, belts, helmets,
shields, chariots, horse trappings, snaffle bits, chains and scale
armour. Fragments of textiles with a fringe of rows of beads were
found at Karmir Blur, as well as 750 tons of carbonised grain and wine
stores with a capacity of 400,000 litres. Quantities of this magnitude
suggest that the fortresses stored all the economic produce of the land,
and not simply the anticipated needs in case of siege. Bronze models
show that many Urartian buildings may have had three storeys or
more, and some have recently been found at Bastam. The lesser
mortals, including the garrison, lived in the lower towns, at Karmir
Blur in spacious courtyard houses arranged in blocks along streets
built on a grid plan. Not much is known about domestic architecture
and much regional variety may be expected to have occurred,
especially as Urartu is a land with many climatic extremes ranging
from the relatively warm and sheltered Araxes valley to the bleak
heights of the Kars plateau or the snowbound mountain lake of Sevan.

We know very little about Urartian trade and industry, but
metalworking would appear to have been Urartu's forte. Bronze
statues of gods and kings were cast, iron was worked and composite
bronze thrones were made with many small figures of deities with
inlaid details. Silver and gold was used for furniture and jewellery,
pins, earrings, pendants etc., some with delicate granulation.
Cauldrons supported by tripods and equipped with handles in the
form of winged human figures, bull's heads or snake-like griffin heads
were exceedingly popular and have a wide distribution outside
Urartu; whether as actual imports or copies they occur in Cyprus,
Gordion, the Greek islands, Delphi, Olympia, Athens and even in
Etruria, where they stimulated local imitation. *Situlae* (buckets) with
lion's or ram's heads found in the royal tomb of Gordias (perhaps the
father of Midas) at Gordion may be of Urartian provenance, as similar
objects are shown as Urartian booty in Sargon's reliefs at Khorsabad,
and earlier examples were discovered at Hasanlu, which was sacked
*c*. 800 BC by the Urartians.

Fragments of ivory furniture, some still overlaid with gold, were
found at Altıntepe, carved in two styles, local Urartian and
Assyrianising. The material, needless to say, was not local but derived
from the gradually dwindling herds of elephants that lived in the

marshier areas around the Orontes River in north Syria, whence ivory had been exported for furniture like that found in the Acemköy Palace since the days of Kanesh Ib, and in the eighth century ivory objects also reached Phrygian Gordion, together with Syrian opaque glass, which has not yet been found in Urartu, but must have been known. Bowls with golden handles from the land of Tabal in central Anatolia were among Sargon's booty from the plunder of the Urartian palace at Ardini, an indication that metalwork travelled both ways. However, far too little is known about contemporary Anatolian kingdoms in Tabal Qué and Phrygia to assess accurately the role of Urartian trade.

Urartian burial customs were varied and comprised both inhumation and cremation, but never burial under tumuli. Royal and princely burials are found in rock-cut chambers, or, where the rock did not allow, built-up stone chambers as at Altıntepe, where the dead rested in stone sarcophagi. A woman would be buried with her jewellery, whereas a man's funeral gifts, chariot parts, weapons and furniture, would be put in an outer room. Associated with the Altıntepe tombs is an open-air sanctuary with a number of plain uninscribed stelae, similar to a shrine of Sardur II at Van with two stelae in niches recording the annals of his reign. Cemeteries of warriors simply buried, but since robbed, have been found near Erebuni and Giyimli, the source of many Urartian bronzes.

Finally we must mention the best known Urartian pottery, the fine red burnished Toprakkale ware, which, with a limited range of shapes, imitates copper vessels and appears to date mainly from the seventh century and is then found from the Euphrates to Lake Urmia and Karmir Blur. What preceded it is still a mystery, which can only be solved by further excavations, but a rarer painted ware occurs at a number of sites. In the Elazig region (not part of Urartu until the reign of Menua) earlier pottery of the Iron Age has been found, handmade or wheel-made buff, red or grey burnished ware with grooved decoration of a rather primitive kind and assigned to *c*. 1100–800 BC; but this cannot be considered as Urartian. The burnished grey ware found in the plain of Muş west of Lake Van shows links with the Iranian Iron Age (*c*. 1350–1000 BC) and may also be a foreign element, as Urartian occupation shunned this area. The origins of the peoples of Urartu evidently reached back into the second millennium BC, to those vaguely termed 'Lands of Hurri' of the Hittite records, but whose archaeology is still a closed book.

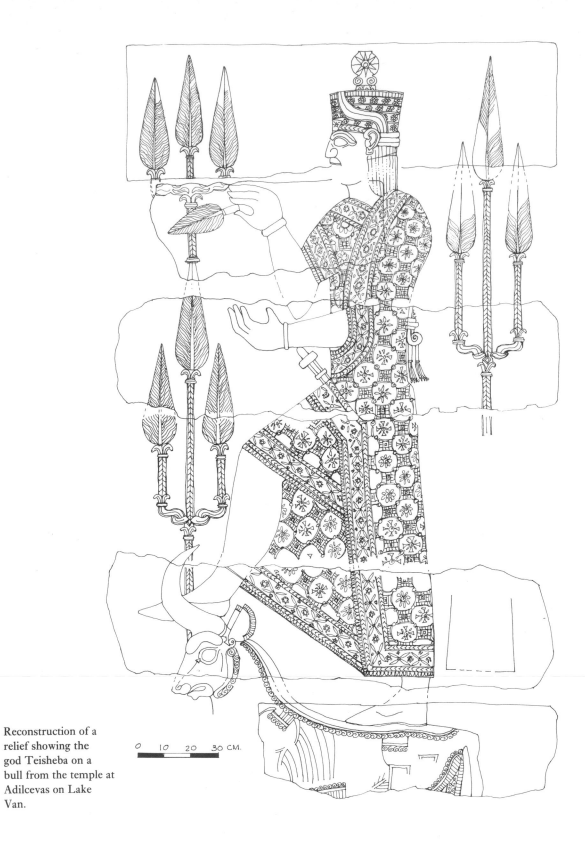

Reconstruction of a
relief showing the
god Teisheba on a
bull from the temple at
Adilcevas on Lake
Van.

0   10   20   30 CM.

# 9

# Lydians and Ionians

During the last century and a half of Anatolian political independence—from the Cimmerian sack of Gordion *c.* 696 to the defeat of Croesus King of Lydia by Cyrus the Persian in 546 BC— Phrygia was succeeded by Lydia as the dominant power in western and central Anatolia. This is another period that eagerly awaits rescue by archaeologists from historical obscurity.

Within a few years of the sack of Gordion, a Lydian noble called Gyges (Gugu) overthrew the dynastic rulers of Lydia, who had probably been Phrygian vassals, and founded a dynasty of his own, around 690 BC. It is known as the dynasty of the Mermnadae, and for five generations its kings were masters of the Phrygian kingdom. They reigned from a new Lydian capital called Sardes, which was reputedly founded by Gyges. Gyges discovered gold in the Pactolus River, just below the citadel, and may have introduced the world's first coinage, in gold, silver and electrum.

Gyges (690–652), after some campaigning against Smyrna and Miletus, was able to establish his protectorate over the Ionian cities, to whom he granted trading rights within his vast domains, which must have benefited them as much as the royal exchequer. Apart from periodical local revolts, the Lydian kings established a tolerable symbiosis with the Ionian and Aeolian Greeks based on mutual respect and self-interest, particularly with Ephesus ('Ipsis' in Lydian), whose oligarchic rulers intermarried with the Lydian royal house. Ephesos contained the chief sanctuary of the kingdom devoted to Artemis, a many-breasted Lydian mother goddess, the original of 'Diana of the Ephesians'. Her cult was administered by a college of priestesses, called 'the bees', and her great Ionian temple, built during the time of the last of the Lydian kings, Croesus, was one of the Seven Wonders of the Ancient World.

Gyges's reign ended in disaster; the Cimmerians, still on the rampage in Anatolia, attacked Lydia, and although Gyges appealed for help from Assyria and Egypt, no help came and he was killed in battle in 652 BC. His capital, Sardes, was plundered and burnt and his kingdom ravished. Nor did the Ionian cities escape; the savage Cimmerian horsemen were depicted on the painted clay sarcophagi of the Clazomenians. Gyges himself was buried in a great tumulus situated across the Hermos River from Sardes at a place called Bin Tepe, the Lydian royal cemetery, which rivalled that of Gordion in funereal magnificence. On the ashlar inner wall of the tomb the name 'Gugu' is engraved in the Lydian alphabet, which was different from Phrygian or Greek.

Unlike the Phrygians the Lydians could claim to be of native Anatolian stock, and their language, though not yet well understood, is of the Hittite-Luwian type. Lydia in fact occupied much the same area as Arzawa proper in the second millennium BC, and though no archaeological continuity can yet be seen at Sardes, it is manifest at Smyrna (Bayraklı). The hieroglyphic script used in the thirteenth century does not seem to have survived the upheaval of *c.* 1200 BC, but the names of the Lydian kings have an unmistakable Luwian flavour. Incidentally, their Ionian and Aeolian neighbours also were mainly of Bronze Age descent, representing refugees from the Mycenaean world, and it is perhaps not surprising that it was in this milieu that Homer composed the *Iliad* and the *Odyssey*, perhaps in Smyrna, or in neighbouring Chios.

Gyges was succeeded by his son, Ardys. Not much is known of his reign, except that he indulged in an eleven-year war with the great Ionian city of Miletos, in western Anatolia. It was perhaps this war, and the fading of the Cimmerian threat, that may have contributed to the growth of Ionian colonisation, mainly by Miletos. Miletos, which already controlled Cyzikus on the Sea of Marmara since *c.* 700 BC, now set out to turn the Black Sea into an Ionian lake, creating a number of Greek colonist cities along its shores.

The Cimmerian menace was finally disposed of by the end of the seventh century. Some time after 640 BC the Assyrians destroyed another Cimmerian army and the next Lydian king, Alyattes (618–566), succeeded in clearing the Cimmerians from his kingdom. During his beneficent reign, Lydia reached the height of its power, but this brought him into conflict with the Medes under Cyaxares.

The Medes, helped by the Babylonians, destroyed the Assyrian Empire in 612 and now expanded westwards, probably overrunning Urartu *c.* 590 BC. A five-year war ensued between Alyattes and Cyaxares, who overran central Anatolia; then on 28th May 585, when the two sides were poised for battle, an eclipse of the sun occurred, and a peace treaty was concluded instead through the mediation of the kings of Babylonia and Hilakku. By the terms of this treaty the Halys River was fixed as the frontier, and Astyages, the crown prince of the Medes, was to marry a daughter of Alyattes. So Lydia was saved, at least for the time being.

Little else is known of Alyattes' 57-year reign, except that he took and destroyed Smyrna. His great tomb, 355 metres in diameter and 69 metres high, stands at Bin Tepe, rivalling the great tumulus at Gordion. It has a stone-lined passage and an inner chamber decorated with fine reliefs of animals, but it was plundered in antiquity.

His son Croesus (561–546), the last Lydian king (and the first Persian satrap of Lydia) is described by Herodotus as an immensely wealthy but tragic figure. He rebuilt Smyrna, established his protectorate over Ephesos, and took Miletos. He sent presents to Delphi and provided the classic example of the foolishness of consulting oracles. 'Cross the Halys and you will destroy a great kingdom,' the oracle told him. So when his brother-in-law, the Median king Astyages, was deposed by Cyrus the Great, the founder of the Achaemenian Empire in Persia, Croesus saw his chance for enlarging his own; he crossed the Halys, only to be defeated by Cyrus at Pteria. He fled back to Sardes where he was defeated once more and taken prisoner by Cyrus and deposed as king, and then reinstalled as Persian governor. The oracle had been careful not to say *which* great kingdom would be destroyed. The year was 546 BC, the end of Anatolian independence.

The Persians ruled Anatolia from 546 till 333 when, at the battle of Issus, Alexander the Macedonian defeated Darius (III) Codomanus, but very little is known of those two hundred years historically or archaeologically. The Persian sources are silent, and the turbulent history of the Athenian league and its Peloponnesian enemies affected only the coastal regions of Anatolia. Persian rule by satraps (governors), of which there were four in the days of Darius—for Ionia (Magnesia), Lydia (Sardes), the south coast (Cilicia), and Cappadocia, and later another in Propontis (Daskylium)—seems on the whole not to have been too much of a burden, if subjects obeyed the Great King and paid the tribute required. If not, they might be

Stone statue of Kybele with flute players from Phrygian Boğazköy.

deported to Lower Mesopotamia, as the people of Miletos were after the Ionian revolt of 499, or to Central Asia or Egypt. Service in the Persian armies may not have been very agreeable, but one does not have the impression that things were quite as bad as under the successors of Alexander, or the Roman Republic, or the Byzantines, when Anatolia was a continuous battlefield and misrule and oppression were the order of the day. That explains why the Seljuk Turks from Iran were eventually welcomed by many of the local population in the eleventh century AD. Still, that was a long way off, and such sentiments may not have been much in evidence in 546 BC, especially not in Lycia on the south coast where the Persian conquest met fierce but short resistance. A century later we find the Lycians fighting on the Persian side against the Greeks and prospering.

The archaeology of this period from *c*. 700–500 BC holds a special fascination in its gradual change of influence between east and west. In the eighth century, Phrygian influence had been predominant with no reciprocal artistic benefits; in the seventh century, in the orientalising style, a sort of mixed Graeco-Lydian culture prevails, and during the sixth century we see the emergence of Ionian beauty, elegance and charm in architecture, sculpture and small objects that captivated and enchanted both Lydians and Persians, and left its mark as much on the reliefs of Xerxes' palace at Persepolis as on the tombs of Lycian nobles at Elmalı, or in Campania, Etruria and Gordion, or in the *kore* statues from the Athenian Acropolis before the Persian destruction in 480 BC.

The high-water mark of Ionian Lydian art of the seventh–sixth centuries BC had its repercussions into the interior of Anatolia, where it met the Phrygian tradition in the region of Yazılıkaya near Midas City at a late Phrygian cult centre of the goddess Kybele Agdistis ('of the rocks') where cult façades, niches and thrones in an eerie rocky terrain among patches of pine forest formed a holy domain where the goddess was thought to manifest herself. Here numerous rock-cut monuments, bearing Phrygian inscriptions, with richly decorated façades surrounding niches in which stood a statue of Kybele, sometime flanked by rampant lions, formed the setting for the open-air cult. Some of these, like the earliest façade, dating from *c*. 600 and inscribed by another Midas, are decorated like the wooden screens from Gordion, whereas others clearly show Phrygian house façades with woodwork details. In the later examples pediments acquire sculptures of evident Ionian inspiration, though some of the earlier ones look like enlarged copies of Lydian ivories. The entire sequence is thought to belong to the sixth century and is 'late Phrygian' in style. The atmosphere of the place is still redolent of sanctity, and one can see why it was chosen. Nor is it surprising, perhaps, that already in the fourteenth century BC an Arzawan ruler, Mashuiluwa, had built a religious city hereabouts, and that there are several hieroglyphic inscriptions in the neighbourhood.

To this period after 700 BC also belongs the reoccupation by 'Late Phrygian' people of the old Hittite capital, Hattusa, which includes fortifications and a city gate outside which in a niche stood a statue of Kybele accompanied by two flute players. Several other more primitive Kybele statues in niches, found in the Ankara region, may belong to this period, as do the impressive mud-brick fortifications of Gordion which were erected after the destruction of the site by the Cimmerians and before the city was rebuilt in the Persian period. Another feature of the Lydian (and possibly Early Persian) period is the use of gaily painted terracotta plaques used as friezes in the decoration of plastered mud-brick buildings. They decorate a

Terracotta plaque with horseman in Ionian style from Düver.

'palace' at Larisa and a possible shrine at Düver near Burdur, and conform very much to Ionian construction including acroteria, spouts, antefixes etc. Plaques of this nature come also from Sardes, Mylasa, and even from as far afield as Pazarlı and Akalan near the Black Sea coast. Their decoration includes formal geometric ornaments as well as friezes with chariot scenes (Larisa), noblemen on horseback (Sardes, Düver), griffins (Düver), clumsily drawn foot soldiers (Pazarlı) and rows of partridges (Mylasa). This form of decoration is evidently a cheaper form of painted relief and may therefore have been popular in the country; its effect is nonetheless charming.

On a less elevated level, the pottery development in the period between 700–500 BC and later clearly lags behind the architecture and sculpture, and no innovations can be observed in the Persian period. Characteristic of the Lydian period are lydions (small, footed jars), drinking bowls, marbled ware and much black on red pottery as well as monochrome and bichrome craters with geometric, floral or animal motifs, much of which looks rather crude compared to the east Greek orientalising ware that dominates the ceramic scene, but which only rarely penetrates far inland. At Gordion the old grey wares continued, together with Greek imports since 650–40, and in the Halys basin, the Pontic coast and the Ankara region, monochrome and polychrome 'late Phrygian' ware prevails, colourful enough, but with debased shapes, and increasingly cruder decoration which now includes animals and human figures, often mere caricatures.

However vigorous the artistic response that peace, trade and, occasionally as in Lycia, participation in the Greek wars may have stimulated, Persian domination in Anatolia, perhaps through its laxity and lack of patronage and interest, encouraged only artistic decline away from the main centres. This is but a supposition, and only further excavation can tell; a conveniently burned satrap's residence with all its treasures preserved would be a boon to archaeology!

# BOOKS FOR FURTHER READING

*General*

AKURGAL, E., Art of the Hittites (London 1962)

ALKIM, U. B., Anatolia, I (London 1969)

BITTEL, K., Die Hethiter (Munich 1976)

Cambridge Ancient History, 3rd edition Vol I, 1 (1970) I, 2 (1971) II, 1 (1973) II, 2 (1975)

METZGER, H., Anatolia II (London 1969)

*Neolithic and Chalcolithic*

MELLAART, J., Çatal Hüyük, a Neolithic Town in Anatolia (London 1967)
    Earliest Civilisations of the Near East (London 1965)
    Excavations at Hacılar (Edinburgh 1970)
    The Neolithic of the Near East (London 1975)

*The Early Bronze Age*

BURNEY, C. A. and LANG, D. M., The People of the Hills. Ancient Ararat and Caucasus (London 1971)

MELLAART, J., The Chalcolithic and Early Bronze Ages of the Near East and Anatolia (Beyruth 1966)

*The Middle Bronze Age*

GARELLI, P., Les Assyriens en Cappadoce (Paris 1963)

ORLIN, L. I., Assyrian Colonies in Cappadocia (The Hague 1970)

ÖZGÜC, T., Kültepe-Kanish (Ankara 1959)

*The Hittites*

BITTEL, K., Hattusha, capital of the Hittites (New York 1970)

HICKS, J., The Empire Builders (New York 1974)

MACQUEEN, J., The Hittites and their Neighbours (London 1975)

*The Iron Age*

AKURGAL, E., *op cit* for the East Luwians

BURNEY, C. A., and LANG, D. M., *op cit* for Urartu

ÖZGÜC, T., Altintepe, 2 vols (Ankara I 1966, II 1969)

PIOTROVSKI, B. B., Urartu (London 1967)

# INDEX